One Man, One God

One Man, One God

The Peace Ministry of Fr Alec Reid C.Ss.R.

Martin McKeever C.Ss.R.

Redemptorist Communications

Published in 2017 by Redemptorist Communications

ISBN: 978-0-9927216-2-6

Printed by ScandBook

Contents

Foreword

The contribution of Fr Alec Reid, Redemptorist, to the Northern Ireland peace process is a story waiting to be told. For so long he was a lone voice calling for dialogue and openness when so many were closed to such a call. For years he worked in the background, in the shadows, helping to create connections that would one day finally bear fruit. We Irish Redemptorists are delighted that at last Alec's story is being told, and we welcome this first book to seek to acknowledge and articulate his extraordinary ministry and commitment, for well over thirty years, to bringing peace not only to Belfast but to the whole country. I believe that the unique value of this particular book is that it is not just a history book simply detailing the events of the Troubles, nor is it just a biography of the life of Alec Reid and of his achievements, but is above all an effort to try to understand what motivated Alec, what inspired him, what kept him going during years of disappointment, frustration and seeming failure. It is a real effort to understand Alec the man, the Christian, the priest. Recently a taxi driver in Belfast, while conducting a tour of the murals in west Belfast, commented that 'If it wasn't for religion there wouldn't have been any troubles in Northern Ireland.' I can certainly understand where this man was coming from and what he meant, but I would also want to claim that if it wasn't for religion and faith we wouldn't have had a peace process. It was above all his faith in Christ and his belief in the power of God's spirit to enable us to overcome evil and hatred that inspired Alec and many other men and women of faith, Catholic and Protestant, to commit their lives to the search for peace. As is clear from his writing, Alec believe that the 'servant of Christ' has a particular contribution to make in the midst of conflict situations; he or she is called to enter into the very midst of such situations and to become agents of dialogue, ministers of communication, and servants of God's justice and compassion. Alec certainly attempted to be all of these things, often at a very real personal cost to his health, and the Lord did great things through him. As Fr McKeever

1

says in the course of this book, 'Alex's faith in Christ, in the power of the Spirit and in the compassionate love of God gave him a different view of a seemingly hopeless situation.'

I take the opportunity of thanking all who make this publication possible. To my Redemptorist colleagues, Fr Michael Kelleher, who was the inspiration and often the driving force behind the project, and Fr Martin McKeever, the author, who has done an excellent job in telling a very complex story. Thanks also to Redemptorist Communications the design and editorial work, and to all who contributed in any way to enabling this production to see the light of day. While this work acknowledges Alec Reid's extraordinary contribution to the peace process in Northern Ireland, we especially hope that the telling of his story will inspire all who work for peace in the many troubled spots in our world, and encourage them never to lose hope or give up, and to continue to dream seemingly impossible dreams, just as Fr Alec did, Christian, priest and Redemptorist.

Dan Baragry C.Ss.R.
Provincial

Preface

In a radio profile of Alec Reid, Olivia O'Leary once said: 'In every conflict there is a no man's land into which few will dare to go. Fr Alec was one who did.' As a phrase, 'no man's land' is said to have first been used to describe parcels of land lying 'just beyond the walls' of London. Alec Reid was a no-man's-land figure, a threshold-man; in his life he traversed the peace-line walls of Belfast.

Alec Reid was a proud Irishman. For many of his generation, being Irish was synonymous with being deeply committed Catholics, 'dyed in the wool' republicans and strong supporters of the Gaelic Athletic Association. Alec was familiar with this understanding, but as anyone who knew him well will testify, his Irish identity was much more complicated. On his father's side, the grandfather after whom he was named Alexander was a Protestant; Alexander did convert for a time to Catholicism in order to marry his Catholic wife, but from census records he would seem to have reverted to his original faith commitment after some years. Alec's mother was a member of Cumann na mBan and a strong republican. Born in Dublin and brought up in Tipperary, Alec was both a Tipp supporter and a Dub! Alec's early history crossed borders.

As a young adult Alec joined the Redemptorists. The Redemptorists were founded in 1732 to preach the Gospel and serve the poorest and most abandoned, those living on the margins. Over the years he dressed in black and wore a Roman collar. Underneath the uniform, however, there were some very deeply held convictions that many in the Vatican might not share – for example, about the role of women in the Church, about the lack of structures to listen to the Holy Spirit working in the Catholic lay faithful; for Alec, priests should get out of their sacristies and work more with and for people 'on the streets'.

Alec was a member of the Clonard community in Belfast for over forty years. From their arrival in Belfast in 1896, the Clonard Redemptorists have

3

worked hard to stay close to the people among whom they live. Alec Reid's peace ministry emerged from a religious community deeply rooted for over a hundred years in the local reality of west Belfast.

In this decade of significant centenaries, it's worth noting here that in 1920 an Irish Redemptorist, Patrick Clune, then an archbishop in Australia, was involved in negotiations between the British government and the Irish Sinn Féin leaders; he conferred with Lloyd George and members of his cabinet and travelled between London and Dublin for several weeks. At the time some Cabinet members were opposed to a truce 'unless the Sinn Féiners delivered up all their arms': the negotiations failed on this question.

During the German bombing of Belfast in 1941, Catholics and Protestants took shelter together in the crypt underneath Clonard church. In the 1970s a Clonard Redemptorist called Christy McCarthy formed a Thursday Bible-study group in which working-class Catholics from west Belfast met with Presbyterian and Anglican members of a middle-class Protestant community. In January 1980 Rev. John Dunlop, a Presbyterian minister, was invited to speak in Clonard. The Clonard/Fitzroy Fellowship began in 1981. The Cornerstone Community was born from a fortnightly prayer meeting of Catholic and Protestant clergy along with lay people, which began to meet in Clonard in the late 1970s. Having held together in commitment to reconciliation during the tensions and pain of the hunger strike, some members set up the community on the Springfield Road in November 1982.

A very significant presence alongside Alec Reid for more than thirty years was his Redemptorist brother Gerry Reynolds, a man deeply committed to friendship and fellowship with Christians of other traditions. On Remembrance Sunday in November 1994, shortly after the IRA ceasefire, Gerry felt the Spirit of God calling him to go into the Shankill to share in the Sunday Morning Service with one of the Protestant congregations there – that was the first 'unity pilgrimage'. Even after the deaths of Alec and Gerry, Clonard unity pilgrims continue to worship with brothers and sisters of other Christian traditions in Belfast and beyond.

My bedroom was opposite Alec's in Clonard in the early 1990s and a memory of that time is of confrères saying he was like the Scarlet Pimpernel – 'we seek him here, we seek him there ... Is he in heaven? Is he in hell? That damned, elusive Pimpernel.' In the early 2000s Alec spent long periods in St Clement's on the Antrim Road, where I was then based. It was at that time that I started to interview him and to record the interviews. Later in that first decade of the 2000s, we were both part of a Redemptorist community in Dublin, and in the last years of Alec's life we spent a considerable amount of time together.

Throughout a very reflective life Alec wrote a great deal unaided. His Aunt Ita was his long-time 'secretary'. In his later years Alec's long-time friend Anne Fitzmaurice and a more recent friend, Eileen Coyne, offered him some secretarial assistance. His sisters Maura and Margaret and various others supported the project of putting his 'Lessons from the Streets' together. His colleague Harold Good heard many versions of the 'Lessons' as they travelled together, making presentations and sometimes receiving awards and honorary doctorates.

During those years various radio and TV programmes were made recording Alec's memories of significant moments in the history of the Troubles. Alec and I worked with some very skilled media folks; those from New Decade and DoubleBand come to mind immediately. In his senior years Alec was not in the best of health, and we very much appreciated when this was handled respectfully and professionally.

In late 2011 we made some of Alec's written material available to Martin McKeever, a Redemptorist professor of moral theology in Rome, and invited him to present and discuss the material at a gathering of clergy from other Christian communities. The material included a paper by Seán O'Riordan, a Redemptorist colleague respected and trusted by Alec and a predecessor of Martin's in Rome. The group gathered in Dromantine in February 2012 to reflect on some of the documents included in this present volume. The material was a revelation to many of the participants. Alec was such a 'shadowy' and unknown figure. Very little, if any, of the material had ever seen the light of day before then.

In 2013 Martin completed two terms as 'preside' of the Alphonsian Academy and dedicated a great part of a sabbatical year to the preparation and writing of this present work. Martin's generous commitment has been remarkable throughout. Since those sabbatical days, Martin's text has benefitted from the feedback of several other Redemptorists and lay people, including Dan Baragry, Peter Burns, Brendan Callanan, Dominic Carroll, Rosemary Gallagher, Gerry Moloney, Máire Ní Cearbhaill and Gerry Reynolds. Patrick O'Donoghue, Michael Brennan and others from Columba Press offered further professional expertise and generous support along the road to publication. Redemptorist Communications was always going to play a significant part in the publishing of this book; I pay tribute here to the excellent work of all the RC team.

In early 2015 Vera Orschel, a professional archivist, joined Antoinette Doran on the Redemptorist provincial staff with a view to bringing greater professional organisation to the 'Alec Reid Archive'. That work is now complete. Vera and others, such as David McNamara, Maura Litster (Alec's sister) and Anne Fitzmaurice, identified photos of interest to be included in this volume. Documents written by Alec that were never made available publicly before are also included here. Though sometimes repetitive, they bear witness to his extraordinary commitment and offer access to Fr Alec's thinking. They are another way of making 'his voice' available to a wider audience.

In the past few paragraphs I have tried to outline as best I can how this book came into being. It was a long and very convoluted process. I wish to acknowledge the contribution of all those mentioned and many others.

Others will write about Fr Alec from different perspectives – historically, politically, religiously; a perspective that does not recognise how Fr Alec understood himself is unlikely to get very far. He saw himself as a servant of Christ in a situation of political conflict. He felt prompted by the Holy Spirit to reach out and work for peace with the folks 'on the other side'. For Fr Alec Christians are 'sent' by God to act in a particular way in the world, depending on their gifts. He often referred to people as 'sent by God'. It seems accurate to say that Alec Reid, Gerry Reynolds (alongside their Clonard colleagues) and many others of different traditions were sent by God to the people of Belfast and beyond during the Troubles. The Redemptorists at Clonard continue to be sent to offer service to God's people in this time.

As a 'no-man's-land man', Alec often spoke about his first visit to Liz, a Presbyterian woman who lived in a house 'on the other side'. Clonard is on the nationalist side, and Liz lived in the Shankill area, on the other side of the 'peace line'. To get to Liz's house from Clonard, Alec had to pass a mural saying 'Welcome to the Loyalist heartland of Ulster.'

His first visit to Liz's house was made after a violent confrontation along the peace line. Although reconciliation was the purpose of his visit, Alec was expecting an angry reception. He knocked on the door. It was opened by a middle-aged woman who looked startled. She drew back in surprise when she realised that he was a priest. He thought she might close the door in his face even before he could explain the friendly purpose of his visit. Instead, she listened to what he had to say and then graciously invited him in.

As he crossed the threshold of what was then to him an alien, even a hostile, world, the first thing he saw was the message that, then, and afterwards, made him feel that, when he was among 'them 'uns' – 'the people on the other side' – he was at home and among friends. There was a wall-hanging placed over the kitchen door. The kitchen, in turn, opened on to the wall of the peace line. Facing out onto the peace line was the message: 'Love One Another'. Suddenly there was a bridge, instead of a gulf, between the people of that house and himself. It was a bridge of common ideals where he could meet in friendship and love.

As he sat down, on that first occasion, to chat, he knew that his mission of peace would be successful. This feeling was confirmed when, on looking around the sitting-room, he saw more emblems of faith and trust in God. One, near the stairs, told him: 'God answers prayers.' Another said: 'The Lord is my Shepherd.' There was also a picture of a vase with roses and the advice: 'Take time to smell the flowers.'

Fr Alec relaxed in that house many times over a cup of tea, looking at the same message of faith, trust and love greeting him from the walls of that room where they were chatting. He learned that those messages were not only proclaimed but also lived in that household. He learned over the years that they are lived, too, in countless, similar Catholic and Protestant households around the Shankill and the Falls.

Liz and Alec became very friendly. One night he phoned her and ended by saying 'Now don't forget to pray for me,' to which she replied: 'You know, every night I pray for you and I blow two kisses over the peace line; a kiss of love and a kiss of peace.'

Alec was granted many honorary doctorates. On receiving some of them he spoke to the graduates about Liz. He recommended to those present that they reach out in friendship to people 'on the other side' in whatever situations they found themselves in life. He left them with some of those words that Liz had on her wall:

> 'Love One Another.'
> 'God answers prayers.'
> 'The Lord is my shepherd, there is nothing I shall want.'
> 'Take time to smell the flowers.'

If Alec were writing this preface he might well used those same words. He would almost certainly have finished by saying 'God bless.' May God continue to bless those who enter no-man's-land, those who cross borders for the cause of peace.

Michael Kelleher C.Ss.R.

Introduction

Every now and then in the history of human affairs, something happens which is of such enormous importance that it is not possible to grasp its significance at the time. Even the main protagonists shaping events and being shaped by them cannot grasp at the time the full import of what they are doing and of what is happening to them. It is only afterwards, in the light of long reflection, that it is possible to understand more fully what it all means.

This would seem to be the case with the event we know as the peace process in Northern Ireland. More specifically, it would seem to be the case with the extraordinary story of the peace ministry of a Redemptorist priest, Fr Alec Reid. Almost twenty years have passed since the signing of the Good Friday Agreement in 1998 and almost fifty since the beginning of this ministry. Since at least 1998 there has been a growing consensus, nationally and globally, that Fr Alec was a figure of major significance. This came out very clearly in the measure and the quality of acknowledgement and appreciation expressed universally at the time of his death in November 2013.

As time goes by, the question arises as to how to recall, understand, preserve and continue this legacy. In a particular way the Dublin province of the Redemptorists, the religious congregation to which Fr Alec belonged, has been wrestling with this question. How can we best honour this figure and at the same time serve the Church and the world as regards peacemaking, particularly in a faith perspective? It gradually became clear that this whole question is so vast and complex that it is not realistic at this point to attempt anything more than a first step. This book is such a first step on the part of the Irish Redemptorists in the ongoing task of assimilating into our collective understanding the significance of the peace ministry in which Fr Alec and others engaged.

It is important that the reader understand from the outset the nature and logic of the book. It is not another history book on the peace process, and it is not a biography. It is, rather, a collection of material that gives us access to the peace ministry of Fr Alec. The various sections of the book contribute to our understanding of this ministry in quite different ways, and need to be read correspondingly. It is hoped that the following overview of the material assembled here will help orientate the reader:

- The first part is an historical essay that outlines in a synthetic fashion what we know about the peace ministry. It is based primarily on long, recorded interviews with Fr Alec and on the vast documentation he left behind.
- The second part is a faith reflection on this peace ministry. The truth is that the preceding historical essay does not tell the full story of Fr Alec because it does not attempt to understand the way in which his ministry was rooted in his faith. This second section is not a continuation of the first part, it is a separate and distinct essay with the specific purpose of reflecting in faith on this peace ministry. To be understood and appreciated it must be read in this light – indeed, read with faith.
- The third section offers a different point of access to the life and work of Fr Alec. It consists in testimonials of individuals who, in quite different ways, remain impressed by this figure. Each testimonial can stand alone, but the cumulative effect is to fill out considerably our appreciation of who Fr Alec was and what he did.
- The fourth section of the book – which contains almost a hundred pages of documentation – requires a particular word of explanation. As we will see presently, writing and editing documents constituted a very large part of Fr Alec's peace ministry. Most of these documents are written in the dense, dry, technical style typical of political negotiation. According to the interests and tastes of the reader, these documents can be examined with more or less attention. From an historical point of view, however, they represent an indispensable source for understanding the political thinking of Fr Alec, and therefore seem to warrant inclusion in this volume.

The story contained and documented in this book has serious implications for all of us. The historical account, the faith reflection, the testimonials and the documents will hopefully serve to draw out these implications for everyone who is committed to peace-building in even the most challenging situations. The Redemptorists are committed to facilitating the ongoing reflection on this ministry not just within the congregation but also with all those interested, especially those of other religious denominations or of other faiths.

Martin McKeever C.Ss.R.

Brief Chronology of the Northern Ireland Conflict, 1969–2005

1965–69	1970–74	1975–79	1980–84	1985–89	1990–94	1995–99	2000–05
• The Troubles' begin (Aug. 1969)	• Internment introduced (9/10 Aug. 1971) • Bloody Sunday (30 Jan. 1972) • Direct rule (28 Mar. 1972) • 'Workers' strike' (15–28 May 1974) • PIRA ceasefire (30 Dec. 1974)	• PIRA ceasefire ends (January 1975)	• Hunger strikes (1981–82)	• Anglo-Irish Agreement (15 Nov. 1985)	• Hume–Adams Joint Statement (24 Apr. 1993) • Downing Street Declaration (15 Dec. 1993) • PIRA ceasefire (31 Aug. 1994) • Quid Pro Quo Accord (6 Sept. 1994) • Loyalist ceasefire (13 Oct. 1994) • Frameworks for the Future (22 Feb. 1995)	• Patrick Mayhew's 'Washington 3' decommissioning method (7 Mar. 1995) • International Body on Decommissioning Report (22 Jan. 1996) • Breakdown of ceasefire (9 Feb. 1996) • PIRA renews ceasefire (19 July 1997) • Sinn Féin enters talks (10 Sept. 1997) • Good Friday Agreement (10 Apr. 1998) • Omagh bomb (15 Aug. 1998) • Hillsborough Declaration (1 Apr. 1999)	• PIRA agrees to decommissioning method (7 Aug. 2001) • Joint Statement by Rev. Harold Good and Fr Alec Reid on Decommissioning (26 Sept. 2005)

Brief Chronology of Fr Alec Reid's Involvement in the Conflict, 1969–2005

1965–69	1970–74	1975–79	1980–84	1985–89	1990–94	1995–99	2000–05
• Pastoral ministry in Clonard Monastery, Belfast (1960s) • Witness to burning of Bombay Street (15 Aug. 1969)	• Prison ministry at Long Kesh (1970s)	• Intervention in republican feud (1975)	• Attempts to dissuade hunger strikers • Illness, stay in Rome, witness to shooting of Pope John Paul II (13 May 1981) • Reinsertion in peace ministry (1981)	• Letter to John Hume (19 May 1986) leads to beginning of talks • Beginning of dealings with Martin Mansergh (1987) • Blessing of dying soldiers (19 Mar 1988)	• Promoting the ceasefire (1994)	• Renewing the ceasefire (1997) • Ministry to the families of the disappeared (1999)	• Joint Statement by Rev. Harold Good and Fr Alec Reid on Decommissioning (26 Sept. 2005)

PART ONE

History

Behind the scenes

The most common way of referring to Fr Alec Reid in republican circles was to use the Irish word for a priest and call him 'The *Sagart*'. Some prisoners in Long Kesh were somewhat less deferential and called him 'Behind the Scenes'. As is often the case, such a nickname captures and caricatures a telling characteristic. For more than twenty years, in fact, Fr Alec worked for peace in secrecy, an indispensable quality if he was to win and keep the trust of the different parties involved. To narrate the history of his role in the Northern Ireland peace process is to tell a story within a story, a secret story within a public story. The wider story is that of the conflict itself, particularly in the period between 1969 and the signing of the Good Friday Agreement in 1998. This is a very long and complicated story that has already been told by different authors with different perspectives.[1] The story within the story is that of Fr Alec's peace ministry. This story has not yet been adequately told, partly because of the secrecy involved.[2] We are fortunate to have an abundance of written and oral sources that can help us overcome this difficulty. The purpose of this piece is to reconstruct this hidden story using these resources, which include extensive recorded interviews with Fr Alec,[3] original documents, existing literature on the peace process, and interviews with other relevant parties.[4]

Before focusing on this hidden story, however, it is historically important to note carefully the relationship between the two stories. A convenient way of doing this is to juxtapose the chronologies of these two stories (see diagram on facing page). Needless to say, both these chronologies represent only a minimal selection of events. The criterion of selection is the relevance of the events to understanding this peace ministry. The cut-off point historically is Fr Alec's involvement in decommissioning in 2005. Study of these chronologies confirms what we know from Fr Alec himself and others involved in the peace process,[5] namely that his involvement took on different forms during different periods. This fact suggests a convenient way of organising this historical account:

Phase I   Ministry in Belfast, 1969–80
Phase II   Re-engagement in Peace Ministry, 1981–94
Phase III   From Ceasefire to Good Friday Agreement, 1994–98
Phase IV   The 'Disappeared' and Decommissioning, 1998–2005

'So that is how this game is played!'

'So that is how this game is played!' was the phrase that passed through Alec's mind as he regained consciousness. He was a young teenager at the time and was playing his first game of hurling when all of a sudden he was charged from the side by a superior force and knocked out. He was never knocked out again, although he played hurling for many years at quite competitive levels. The trick was to be quick enough with your shoulder so as not to be there when the superior force arrived. This anecdote Fr Alec Reid recounted from his boyhood days will serve us as a kind of symbolic introduction to a character who was to remain on his feet on the tough playing fields of political conflict for over thirty years.

Political context

Since the creation of Northern Ireland in 1921, the division between the majority Protestant community (loyalists or unionists), who generally regard themselves as British, and the significant Catholic minority (republicans or nationalists), who generally regard themselves as Irish, had been a running sore of tensions and discrimination. By the mid-1960s, 'civil rights' were increasingly a moral and political cause on the international scene, most notably in the campaigns led by Martin Luther King in the United States. A similar form of awareness and protest amongst Catholics began to emerge gradually in Northern Ireland in the mid-1960s.[6] This was enough to provoke a violent reaction on the part of some fringe loyalists. When the protest movement took on the form of organised peaceful marches, these were met with violence on the part of loyalists and the Royal Ulster Constabulary (RUC). This phase also provoked direct, violent attacks on Catholic homes, including some close to Clonard Monastery in Belfast where Fr Alec was living. By the early 1970s, violence had grown to such proportions that the British government decided to establish direct rule (1972), which was to remain in place until the Good Friday Agreement in 1998. Before taking up the story in more detail from Fr Alec's point of view it will be useful to review the key political developments in each of the 'camps' involved during these years.

Within Northern Ireland, the unionist camp saw a succession of prime ministers: Terence O'Neill, James Chichester-Clarke and Brian Faulkner. O'Neill's efforts at reform proved to be 'too little, too late'. The mainstream unionist position gradually hardened in the face of rising violence. Faulkner's decision to resort to internment in 1971 was destined to alienate many in the nationalist community. The more radical side of unionism throughout this period was symbolised by Ian Paisley and his Democratic Unionist Party (DUP), which was founded in 1971. Efforts, involving the unionists, to establish a power-sharing Executive in Northern Ireland in the light of the Sunningdale initiative were eventually blocked by the 'workers' strike' of 1974. The rift between unionists and loyalists that was to be so crucial in the later phases of the peace process was thus already in evidence in the 1970s.

On the nationalist side an important political development was the founding, in 1970, of the Social Democratic and Labour Party (SDLP), led first by Gerry Fitt and then, for many years, by John Hume. Within republicanism, the split between the Official and the Provisional IRA was soon followed by a split between Official and Provisional Sinn Féin. Despite an IRA ceasefire in 1974 and talks between the IRA and William Whitelaw (then Northern Ireland secretary), no agreement was reached, and the IRA proceeded with its campaign, albeit in a much more discriminating fashion than before.

The 1970s in Britain saw first the election of Edward Heath, then that of Harold Wilson, and finally that of Margaret Thatcher (1979). Clearly, a key relationship under direct rule was that between the British prime minister and the secretary of state for Northern Ireland. A series of individuals occupied this trying position in the course of the decade, and brought to it their particular strengths and limitations: William Whitelaw, Merlyn Rees, Roy Mason and Humphrey Atkins.

On the Dublin front, the 1970s saw the predominance of Fianna Fáil, first under Jack Lynch and then under Charles Haughey. Shocked by the scale of the violence and perplexed as to what to do if it escalated further, the Southern government could do little more than look on as events unfolded. In August 1971, however, Heath met Lynch and Faulkner at Chequers, an early indication of the importance of what was to become known as the 'totality of relationships' between the parties involved.

One factor that was to make Fr Alec's peace ministry so difficult was the number of parties involved and the range of political opinion between them. Not only this, but each camp was changing from within all the time, so that to reach agreement it was necessary not only to have a degree of consensus among the different groups but to have it at a certain point in time and to attempt to hold onto it as circumstances changed. Fr Alec's ministry consisted in part in overcoming the political paralysis induced by this complex mesh of relationships by opening lines of communication where they did not exist.

Early days in Belfast

When Fr Alec was appointed to the Redemptorist Community at Clonard Monastery in the early 1960s,[7] he became a member of a religious community that already had close ties to the surrounding area.[8] Clonard was not a parish but provided a base for pastoral missions, a retreat ministry and publications, both locally and over a wider area. The site upon which the monastery was built in 1899 lies within a working-class area of Belfast inhabited predominantly by Catholics, but bordering on a working-class Protestant area. In the decades since the creation of Northern Ireland in 1921, there had been occasional vicious pogroms, some of them in the vicinity of Clonard. Over the decades a certain relationship had developed between the Redemptorists and the local, and indeed not so local, people.[9] In the 1960s the huge metal security barriers known as the peace line did not yet exist, but there were deep political, cultural and religious divisions between the local people. Despite these divisions, Clonard had served as a place of encounter between Catholics and Protestants. These encounters took on different forms in different periods: sharing the protection of the church's vault during the air raids of the Second World War, a 'Mission to non-Catholics' that began in 1948, a Bible study group in the 1970s, and more recently such ecumenical groups as the Cornerstone Community and the Clonard/Fitzroy Fellowship.

During the 1960s Fr Alec was involved in various pastoral ministries in the Clonard area, as well as pastoral work in other parts of Ireland. His primary task was to work on a Redemptorist magazine called at the time the *Redemptorist Record* (currently entitled *Reality*). Holding an honours degree in English from University College, Galway, he must have seemed to his superiors a suitable choice for a job that involved writing. What his superiors could not have known was that over the next thirty years Fr Alec would spend a great deal of his time writing political reports, commentaries and position papers with, for and to (according to the occasion) the major parties involved in the peace process. Indeed, a substantial part of Fr Alec's contribution to the peace process consisted in his active participation in the drafting of such documents.[10]

One day, while at the monastery reception desk during his earliest days in Clonard, Fr Alec met a Traveller boy (Travellers are an itinerant ethnic group). As a result of this personal contact he grew increasingly aware of the often difficult conditions of the Travellers, particularly of their children, and the struggles they faced. As a result, he undertook, with others, various social initiatives on their behalf – an early sign of his sensitivity to human distress and his readiness to get involved concretely and politically in order to relieve it.[11] Interestingly, some of his first contacts with political authorities in Northern Ireland were by way of seeking funds for Travellers.[12]

Apart from such specific pastoral tasks, from the very beginning a more general relationship of deep affection grew between Fr Alec and the local people. Over the years he developed a profound admiration for the faith of the ordinary working-class Catholic women of west Belfast. Reflecting on these years in hindsight, he comments:

> I would say the best Catholics in the world are Belfast Catholics, you know and Northern Ireland Catholics … it's in their guts, you know? Now I go on a pilgrimage every year with a group from west Belfast. I've been doing it for thirty-five or thirty-six years … basically the same group … And if you want to renew your faith, you know, all you have to do is to be with them, just be with them because, I mean, it's just, it's like … like the sun shining, kind of … it's as natural to them.[13]

One of the questions people often ask about Fr Alec is how did he keep going? Part of the answer is to be found in these words and what they tell us about the way in which he received inspiration from the local people. One can sense here how he absorbed the faith of the local people in such a way that it became his own.[14] In the long, dark years ahead this was to remain a vital source of personal spiritual nourishment.

Another extremely important dimension to Fr Alec's pastoral ministry in these early years was the personal contact he had with the Protestant community at different levels. At the time another member of the Clonard community, Fr Hugh Arthurs, was engaged in a form of ministry to

'non-Catholics'. This ministry opened the way for a gradually developing involvement of Clonard in ecumenism. Through activities such as the
Christian Unity Week, ecumenical meetings in Glenstal and Corrymeela,
and annual ecumenical outings to ancient sites, Fr Alec gradually became
more aware of ecumenism as a cause and more familiar with other religious
denominations in Northern Ireland.

Even more significantly he gradually got to know and appreciate ordinary
Protestant people, and even loyalist paramilitaries who were not so interested
in ecumenism! This happened partly at his own spontaneous initiative and
partly through a network of contacts that gradually developed. The personal
initiative took the form of going over the peace line to talk to Protestants
in their own area:

> I remember going into one of those streets one day ... there
> must have been some trouble ... I remember doing that. Going
> to those streets ... and saying to them ... 'Look, there is no plot
> of any kind among the nationalists to attack ye or attack your
> street here' and I remember one of them saying to me: 'You'd be
> welcome in ninety-nine per cent of the houses in this street' ...
> So experiences like that taught you, you see, I remember that well
> and it would help you to form your attitude towards the loyalists.

As regards more formal contacts with loyalist paramilitaries, these were
facilitated by a Catholic businessman, who very early on in the Troubles
saw the need for opening up communication with these groups. These
early contacts, which in some cases even became friendships,[15] were very
important later in the Troubles when the loyalist paramilitaries became more
interested in making peace and were in search of those they could trust in
dialogue.[16]

It is important to recognise from the beginning that Fr Alec did not
arrive in Belfast politically neutral. Although he was normally very discreet
about expressing it publicly, he had inherited from his mother[17] a strong
propensity towards republicanism.[18] While categorically against the use of
violence (even that of the 1916 Rising),[19] he had a better understanding
of where republican violence comes from than most people. This being
the case, it is not difficult to understand his strong reactions to the injustices inherent in Northern Ireland from the outset.[20] Nor is it difficult to

understand his presence at some of the early civil rights marches, something that could not be said of many other priests living in Belfast at that time.

The Troubles

The Troubles of August 1969 descended on west Belfast, on Clonard Monastery and on Fr Alec like a bombshell. As it happens he was in the monastery, looking out on the Protestant mobs, on the afternoon the burning of Bombay Street took place. He was thus a direct eyewitness to some of the most traumatic violence at the very beginning of the Troubles. It is worth quoting his memories of that day:

> Well, I was watching it. I remember I was looking out of the top floor of the monastery and I saw them coming in because you could look down Bombay Street ... And I remember looking out and seeing the loyalists coming in with petrol bombs and guns and throwing petrol bombs into the houses. They went down the street and they burnt about two thirds of Bombay Street ... And the big thing was that they were going to burn the monastery as well, you see. At least that is what we were told ...
>
> ... I was looking out from the top floor of the monastery and as I did I saw this young man about sixteen or seventeen down at the end of Waterville Street at the corner of Bombay Street and the loyalists were coming up ... I think he may have thrown some bricks and then saw they had guns ... he turned and ran and, of course, when he turned and ran they opened fire on him and shot him in the back. And I was watching all this from the top corridor and they were just down from me on Waterville Street and I saw him running down the street about one hundred yards and then collapsing, at a lamppost I remember ... so I decided I would go down to help him, pick him up or see what was going on, and I went down into Waterville Street and there was shooting, it was dangerous I remember ... Well, when I got out on the street ... Fr Pat Egan and these two lay people appeared from the left-hand side of the street and they were running down the footpath and they got to him before I got to him ... now I didn't know if he was dead or alive and it's only afterwards that I was told that he had died ... When I came in after Gerald

McCauley, I went up into the chapel and knelt down and began
to pray that we'd be safe …

This is the first of many circumstances in which Fr Alec would find himself
in dangerous situations of violence in Northern Ireland. The same man who
spent hours and hours of his life drafting quite technical political documents did not hesitate to expose himself to danger when he decided he
must help someone else in danger or in trouble. On one occasion, when
he was heading out with Rev. Ken Newell to a dicey meeting with loyalist
commanders and his friend expressed some doubt about the wisdom of the
venture, Fr Alec's response was 'in for a penny, in for a pound'.[21]

Such events could not but have a major impact on the Clonard area.
Fr Alec reports that local people bitterly complained that they had been
abandoned by the IRA.[22] Within a matter of months the IRA assumed the
role of defending Catholic areas from attacks. Once the British government
decided to send troops onto the streets, the IRA saw these as 'legitimate
targets' within the century-old battle for the reunification of Ireland. Add
to this a policy of internment (1971), which saw many nationalists detained
without trial, and one can begin to understand the kind of tensions building
up around Clonard, and throughout Northern Ireland, in the 1970s. It only
needed Bloody Sunday (30 January 1972)[23] to confirm the conviction of
many within republicanism that armed force was the only way forward. The
situation became even more volatile when the IRA engaged in a bombing
campaign, including the terrible 'Bloody Friday' bombings of July 1972, and
loyalist paramilitaries retaliated with the random assassination of Catholics.

Within this emerging, dramatic, wider story of the conflict, Fr Alec and
his confrères in Clonard had to decide how to respond. The position of the
institutional Church, as represented particularly by Bishop Cahal Daly, was
one of condemnation of IRA and loyalist violence, but of scarce attention to
the forms of violence being used by the state. As we shall see later, Fr Alec
became sharply aware of the limitations of such an approach, and decided
that an alternative was needed.

A key element in shaping this alternative pastoral approach was direct
contact with violence on the ground. In the early 1970s riots in Catholic
areas were almost daily occurrences. Rather than judge what was happening
from a safe distance, Fr Alec made a point of going to the people who were
rioting and trying to understand why they were doing so:

I remember the first riot I ever went to and I noticed a young man in a white shirt who was leading the charge. They were attacking with bottles and bricks or stones, because the British army would shoot you if they saw you with a petrol bomb. But I discovered the leader of this riot had, two years before, been our senior altar boy ... That taught me to be careful, not to condemn riots out of hand but to try to find out what was the cause behind them.

In a similar vein, it is important to know that quite early on in the Troubles, Fr Alec, on his personal initiative, decided to seek contact with the IRA. In the first instance this was with a view to trying to persuade them to desist from violence in the local area, which also endangered the lives of non-involved civilians.[24] As time went on, particularly through his prison ministry, these early contacts turned into solid relationships, which were to prove crucial for the peace process.

Prison ministry
It is impossible to understand Fr Alec's peace ministry in the 1980s without appreciating the grounding importance of his prison ministry in the 1970s. For some years this took the form of weekly visits, Sunday Eucharist, and contact with the prisoners' families.

My prison ministry began, first of all, with the time of internment. You'd get in your car, you'd drive down and you'd go through the process of going through security ... There was one prisoner who used to come up to me every Sunday and he was in the INLA. Every Sunday he came up to me, I don't know why he did but he did; we'd have a chat; he wasn't from Belfast but from down the country. And, afterwards, when I saw the photographs of the ones who had died on hunger strike, he was one of them, I recognised his face ... Bobby Sands used to come up to me, too, in his position as second in command, and I used to have conversations with Bobby standing at the altar. Now, it was very funny: some of them would want to go to confession. I used to put on an alb before Mass and I'd sit down in a chair behind the altar as the prison officers ... would be looking in these little windows ...

In the mid-1970s an extremely important development took place for our understanding of Fr Alec's emerging role. He and a respected Belfast priest, Fr Des Wilson, became involved in the settling of feuds between rival factions of republican paramilitaries. Of particular significance was a feud between the Official and the Provisional IRA in 1975. On this occasion Gerry Adams asked Fr Alec to intervene.[25] This form of contact, along with the reputation he had developed in prison ministry, formed the basis of Fr Alec's unique relationship with republicans in later phases of the peace process. A key concept used at this time to capture the nature of this ministry was that of 'sanctuary'. Before becoming a place where people of different religious and political traditions could meet, Clonard Monastery in the 1970s had already been a setting for reconciliatory meetings between feuding republicans. As the decade wore on, however, the situation became much more tense. A key issue was the political status of the prisoners and their refusal to wear prison clothes. Fr Alec was to find himself at the very centre of this major problem.

One of his contacts on this issue was Cardinal Ó Fiaich.[26] A native of Crossmaglen, the cardinal was overtly more 'republican' in his vision than most Northern clerics. He visited Long Kesh in 1978 and observed, to his horror, the conditions there. Together with Bishop Edward Daly he was active in trying to persuade the British authorities, particularly Margaret Thatcher, that concessions on the clothing question would be much preferable to the kind of reaction the threatened hunger strikes would provoke. Despite some false promises, nothing came of these efforts, and in the end the hunger strikes went ahead.

Fr Alec was active in trying to dissuade the republicans from proceeding with the hunger strikes. It is worth hearing his direct account of these distressing circumstances:

> So I went to see Bobby Sands when I heard of the hunger strike and I spent an hour and a half trying to persuade Bobby Sands not to allow the hunger strike to go ahead, and I remember he got into a state of shock, that was a strange thing ... We were talking for about an hour and a half and for the last half hour he was going like that [shaking], and I said to myself I'm putting too much pressure on this man ... I had better stop. Now I regret I did but I decided to stop after an hour and a half ...

I remember when I came out after talking to Bobby Sands – as I said, you had to be taken out – there was a minibus that took you from whatever part of the prison you were in, out to the gate – I was waiting for this minibus and I must have been waiting for a good half an hour and I got the feeling … I felt sick and I never had been sick, but I remember walking up and down … two or three days afterwards I conked out and I was taken to hospital … And that was the end … the hunger strike went on and I was out …

Fr Alec's collapse and subsequent hospitalisation marked an abrupt end of his activities at this point. One of Fr Alec's visitors in hospital was Gerry Adams, who helped maintain some kind of link between Fr Alec and the people he had been serving in his prison ministry.[27]

A time of rest in Rome!

The first part of Fr Alec's involvement in the conflict finished when he fell ill with some kind of nervous exhaustion at the very beginning of the hunger strikes. He had to be moved out of Belfast. Against his wishes his Redemptorist superiors convinced him to go to Rome. As fate would have it, he was actually close to John Paul II when he was shot in St Peter's Square in 1981:

So, anyway, the Pope was going around in his Popemobile and as he arrived they all started to jostle one another to get a photograph … he had just passed me and there was a bang that turned out to be a shot. I recognised it was a shot and all the pigeons up in the Bernini colonnade there, they all started to fly all over the place … But just after the shot rang out, for some reason I turned around and there was a fellow, foreign-looking, about, I'd say, in his late twenties or early thirties and he was jumping up and down and waving his hands in the air, kind of shouting 'Hallelujah'. The next thing one of the Swiss Guard jumped at top speed over the barrier and I was the last one at the barrier because at the shot everybody had run … there was a picture on the front of *Time* magazine showing the Pope with this person who had tried to shoot him and I recognised him as the fellow I had seen jumping up and down.

Of the many strange and dramatic things that happened in Fr Alec's life, this is surely one of the most remarkable. A worn-out peacemaker priest comes to Rome to rest and is a close eyewitness of an attempt to assassinate the Pope! Incredible as it may seem, this incident is in some ways not an inappropriate way of concluding this phase of Fr Alec's peace ministry: a dramatic encounter between faith and violence.

'Somebody has got to do something about this'

'Somebody has got to do something about this', as we shall see below, is what Fr Alec said to himself before deciding to become engaged in a more politically significant way in the peace process in the early 1980s. Before getting to this point he had to gradually understand the nature of the political problem and try to discern an appropriate pastoral response. It was a complex challenge.

The political context

The most important consequence of the hunger strikes of 1980–81 was the emergence of Sinn Féin as a political force. The election of republicans during and after the hunger strikes had revealed the beginning of a shift in the Northern nationalist constituency away from the more moderate parties towards the more militant positions of Sinn Féin. For those within the organisation who were convinced of the need for an alternative strategy to that of violence, electoral success was a crucial factor.

As time went on, a similar dynamic became evident on the loyalist side: the main paramilitary organisations developed political wings that eventually became new political forces. Like their republican counterparts, many members of these paramilitary organisations had spent time in jail and had reflected critically on the past while trying to envisage a better future for themselves, their families and their community.[28] All along, members of the Protestant clergy, such as Presbyterian minister Roy Magee, had been talking with these groups about the possibility of peace. By the early 1990s, after two decades of hardship, some of these men and women were more capable of flexibility and openness in their political thinking than their mainstream colleagues. Concretely, from the Ulster Volunteer Force (UVF) emerged the Progressive Unionist Party, while from the Ulster Defence Association (UDA) came the Ulster Democratic Party, both of which were to be important in ensuring a loyalist ceasefire and thus reaching the Good Friday Agreement.

In Britain this was the decade of Margaret Thatcher. Her stance on the hunger strikes proved to be very much a hollow victory since probably no other single factor contributed more to the emergence and eventual triumph of Sinn Féin as a political force.[29] Despite her reluctance, the prime minister was eventually persuaded to sign the Anglo-Irish Agreement of 1985. With the arrival of John Major in 1990, and particularly with that of Peter Brook as Northern Ireland secretary, the British approach to Northern Ireland became visibly less high-handed. After long, unfruitful efforts at peace talks, Peter Brooke is most remembered for his public declaration concerning British policy on Northern Ireland, which anticipated the crucial Downing Street Declaration of 1993.

In the South of Ireland the key political figures in this period were Charles Haughey and Garret FitzGerald, who exchanged places several times as Taoiseach and leader of the opposition. Haughey was in principle open to peace initiatives, but was very wary of direct contact with Sinn Féin. Garret FitzGerald, who was much concerned with limiting Sinn Féin's political expansion, was co-signatory of the significant Anglo-Irish Agreement of 1985. The return of Charles Haughey to office in 1987 considerably increased the possibilities of winning the support of the Dublin government for a combined nationalist alternative strategy. Matters accelerated when Albert Reynolds took over from Charles Haughey as leader of the Dublin government in 1992. The political high point of this period of the peace process was the Downing Street Declaration of 1993, signed by Major and Reynolds, which included the principle of agreed self-determination for Northern Ireland. Vital to the achievement of the IRA ceasefire in 1994 was the so-called Quid Prod Quo Accord, according to which the IRA would cease violence in return for Sinn Féin's participation with the Southern government and the SDLP in a common nationalist alternative strategy.

Rethinking peace ministry

When Fr Alec returned to Belfast after his illness in 1981, it was on condition that he would stay out of peace ministry for health reasons. At a time when religious superiors sometimes had difficulties persuading people to go north, the problem with Fr Alec was trying to persuade him to stay south. Recognising that, paradoxically, living in the North was necessary for his psychological health, in that he could not be at peace with himself elsewhere, Fr Alec's doctor suggested a compromise: other forms of ministry in Belfast. This unlikely scenario lasted for some time, during which Fr Alec reports that he responded negatively to requests from republicans to become involved again in peace ministry.[30]

Then, in October 1981, he was approached by an IRA member about an Ulster Defence Regiment (UDR) soldier, Tommy Cochrane, who had been kidnapped. The IRA member explained that he had the authority to have this man's life spared, but that this meant travelling to South Armagh and he did not wish to do so alone. Fr Alec agreed to accompany him, but when they got there it was too late – the man had been killed.

Stung by this new death and this failure,[31] Fr Alec approached Gerry Adams to see if there was any way of avoiding more deaths. The account he gives of these early conversations with Gerry Adams is seminal for understanding this phase of his involvement in the peace process. He reports as follows the response he received from Adams: 'The only organisation that can do anything is the Church – the Church is the only organisation that has the status, the credibility, the lines of communication.'

Right through the 1970s Fr Alec had been struggling with the question as to the right role for the Church in this conflict situation. The conviction of Gerry Adams in 1981 about the role of the Church was vital in pushing Fr Alec towards assuming a more proactive role than in the previous decade.

It is worth pausing for a moment here to consider the significance of this question. We must remember that, at this time, Fr Alec, by his own wish, was nobody in the political life of Northern Ireland. He was 'a wee priest' who visited prisoners and their families. He had not been asked by the bishop or by his Redemptorist superiors to initiate a peace process.[32] Indeed, for health reasons he was expected to stay out of politics. Despite his good intentions, Fr Alec was not able to do so, and within a year of returning to Belfast he not only became involved again but set out ('a one-man peace process', in the words of Irish journalist Ed Maloney) to do something about the situation. And yet all that he does, he does as a priest and as a Redemptorist.[33] To understand him we have to distinguish between the complete sincerity and utter dedication with which he exercised his ministerial role and his somewhat ambiguous position vis-à-vis Church authorities, including Redemptorist ones. This second point will come up again and again in the following years.

The ambiguity of Fr Alec's position consisted in the fact that, on the one hand, he needed to have his hands free if he was going to be effective in his delicate role, but that, on the other hand, he needed to be able to claim that he was acting in the name of the Church.[34] He was indeed acting in the name of the Church in that it was as a Redemptorist and as a priest that he was doing what he was doing.[35] He had at least the tacit approval of his religious superiors and that of at least some members of the Catholic hierarchy, including the cardinal of Armagh. There was also an element of political pragmatism involved here: Fr Alec knew that it would be easier for parties to accept an invitation to talks at which their adversaries would be present if invited by someone representing the Church.

As regards the sincerity of his approach, this finds expression in this moving account of his decision to engage more actively in the political dimensions of peace ministry:

> So I went along one night to a wake in a house in the Clonard area ... it was the wake of an innocent nationalist who was shot by the loyalists because, as I've said, we had this practice of going to all the funerals and wakes of anybody who had been shot like that. So I was there, anyway ... I was kneeling down saying the rosary with them, and the next thing this woman – to my memory she was a young woman of about thirty – went over to the coffin and she started to *caoineadh*, you know the Irish word *caoineadh* [to keen]. It was keening [traditional wailing lament] anyway, she was leaning over the coffin and I said to myself, now it was really heartrending to listen to it, and I remember saying there's something wrong here, something wrong with our society that anybody living in it would have to go through this kind of suffering ... And then I remember saying to myself something's got to be done about this. Somebody has got to do something about this because this is not right ... then I remember thinking I have to do something about this, it was almost the same thought.

This is probably the most intimate statement we have of Fr Alec's decision to engage in a new form of peace ministry. He, like other priests, was already involved in visiting prisoners and their families. What we have here is a decision 'to do something about this' in the sense of adding to ordinary pastoral ministry an effort to engage actively with the political players involved in the conflict. It was Gerry Adams who again offered insight on how this might be done:

> I remember I went to Gerry at the Sinn Féin office in Andersonstown and I sent word that I wanted to see him and

he must have sent word for me to go up there. And I remember
he was sitting on his hunkers outside the main door of the Sinn
Féin office and I was standing with my back to the wall and I was
saying: 'What can you do to stop the IRA? Can anything be done
to stop the IRA?' because, you see, our objective was to stop people
being killed and our first objective was to stop our own people
killing, that was the IRA. I remember he directed me then and he
said: 'There's only one way you are going to stop the IRA, only one
way and that is to get a peaceful strategy that is credible to them
and to be credible to them it will have to be a common nationalist strategy.' In other words, he said, 'a strategy that involved Sinn
Féin, the SDLP and the Irish government …'

Taken together with the previous comment, in hindsight this statement goes
a long way towards explaining Fr Alec's contribution to the peace process.
Having been affirmed in his conviction that the Church should be doing
more, he is now given an idea about what concretely could be done.[36]

Between the early 1980s and the ceasefire of 1994, and then again before
the Good Friday Agreement, a large part of Fr Alec's work consisted in
facilitating communication between the nationalist parties with a view to
agreeing an alternative strategy.[37]

A letter to John Hume
The obvious place to begin any effort at constructing such a strategy was
with the Social Democratic and Labour Party – a nationalist political party.
Early attempts to make contact with the deputy leader, Seamus Mallon, had
proved frustrating and ultimately unsuccessful. As a kind of last attempt,[38]
Fr Alec then decided to write a long letter directly to John Hume, the
leader of the party. This is such an important document that it warrants
close attention.

A good case can be made for considering this letter a turning point in the
peace process. If we include in the peace process, as we surely must, all the
preliminary work done by Fr Alec and his colleagues in the period between
1969 and 1986, then this letter can be seen as a kind of bridge between that
work, and a new, decisive phase in the peace process.

It is important to remember that this letter, dated 19 May 1986, was
written quite soon after the announcement of the Anglo-Irish Agreement

signed by Margaret Thatcher and Garret FitzGerald in November 1985. The SDLP welcomed this announcement, whereas Sinn Féin responded sceptically. In addition to this specific issue, there was broader dissent between the SDLP and Sinn Féin. They were political rivals for the nationalist vote, although at this time Sinn Féin was very much a lesser political force. Along with the British and Irish governments, the various Church authorities and the other main political parties, the SDLP insisted that there could be no negotiations with Sinn Féin while violence continued. These factors taken together made this a peculiarly delicate moment for a mediator like Fr Alec to attempt to establish direct contact between the SDLP and Sinn Féin.

These difficulties help us to understand the tone and objective of the letter. The tone moves from being personal and cordial to being political and pragmatic. At the beginning Fr Alec is at pains to explain the nature of his interest in the problem:

> I would like, first, to explain that my interest is not political but pastoral and moral … I believe that a priest, again like the Church herself, must respond to the human and moral dimensions of a political situation, especially insofar as it involves people, whoever they may be, in suffering and tragedy … My only aim is to help those who, if the present situation continues, will be killed, injured or imprisoned over the next few weeks or months.

Fr Alec goes on to explain the kind of ministry he has been engaged in, particularly among republicans. He then makes the following statement: 'As we went along we could see, to our great surprise, a whole scene opening up in which ways to a true and lasting peace were beginning to define themselves.'

The full significance of this key statement can be better appreciated if we take what is said here together with what Fr Alec recalls about his early attempts at peace ministry. One of his most important realisations was that, as he puts it, 'we were pushing an open door'.[39] He goes on to explain in this interview that both because of the gradual realisation that the policy of 'armed struggle' was not bringing political progress and because of the hardships involved for their families and themselves, many people within the IRA were interested in alternative solutions.

The tone of the letter now changes, and Fr Alec outlines the key proposal:

The essence of this proposal is that the Nationalist parties, north
and south, would agree, through dialogue between themselves,
to formulate and, then, to co-operate in a common Nationalist
policy of aims and methods of resolving the conflict and establishing a just and lasting peace.

If we remember the way in which Fr Alec reported his first meetings with
Gerry Adams after his renewed engagement with the political problem, we
can recognise this as a more technical formulation of the same key idea.

The importance of the figure of Gerry Adams finds expression in the
letter in a long excursus in which Fr Alec is at pains to explain to John
Hume that the position of Adams is not as unreasonable as often depicted.
To this end Fr Alec reports extensively a taped commentary he received
from a renowned Redemptorist moral theologian, Fr Seán O'Riordan, on an
open letter written by Gerry Adams to Bishop Cahal Daly. The key points
made by Fr O'Riordan that Fr Alec wishes to emphasise to John Hume
are that Gerry Adams and others are genuinely interested in an alternative to violence and that they should in any case be listened to. The fact of
quoting another Church figure, and an eminent moral theologian at that,
gives weight to Fr Alec's insistence that the Church has the pastoral responsibility to facilitate the search for an alternative strategy to that of violence.
Finally, Fr Alec gets around to stating his primary objective, which is that of
inviting, in the name of the Church, both the SDLP and Sinn Féin to meet.

Towards the end of the letter we find this atypical statement, one of the
few in which Fr Alec speaks of his role:

I am certain that, if the situation is handled properly, the IRA
can be persuaded to end their campaign. I am not saying this
lightly but from long experience of dealing with the Sinn Féin
movement. Although I am not, and never have been associated
with them in a political sense, as they themselves would testify, I
know that they trust me and understand that any contacts I have
had with them were always in the context of ending violence and
making peace. In this contact, I have, I believe, had closer and
more continual contact with them than any other priest and,
perhaps, any other individual outside their own movement. I
believe, therefore, that I can sense opportunities for making peace

and I know that I can sense an opportunity now in the context
of the approach I have set out in this letter.

It is hard to overestimate the political significance of these statements taken
together in the context of this letter. At a time when the two main nationalist groupings in Northern Ireland are alienated from each other, a Catholic
priest writes to one of the leaders. Having declared the nature of his interest
and illustrated the kind of ministry he has been engaged in, he shares the key
idea of uniting the different nationalist traditions with a view to changing
the political equation and facilitating a lasting solution. Knowing the difficulties this would present for John Hume, he proposes concrete steps,
involving the Church as an intermediary. Most of all, he can claim with
authority that there is a real hope for peace if this strategy is adopted.

We can easily imagine the dilemma all this posed for John Hume.
Publicly committed to the broadly accepted idea that no dialogue with
Sinn Féin was possible while violence continued, how could he accept this
invitation? If a person in the position of Fr Alec was telling him that peace
was possible and offering a strategy for promoting it, how could he refuse
it? To his eternal credit, John Hume responded almost immediately to Fr
Alec in declaring his willingness to cooperate, despite the obvious political
risks involved.[40] Before proceeding with this story, it is important to recount
some significant intervening developments.

Blessing the dying corporals
Quite early on in the prolonged period of contacts that were born of the
letter to John Hume occurred the dramatic incident that made Fr Alec
known worldwide. The background to the event was the killing of three IRA
Volunteers in Gibraltar on 6 March 1988 followed by a gun and grenade
attack at their funeral by Michael Stone (a loyalist member of the UDA),
killing three people. On 19 March 1988 at the funeral of Kevin Brady, one
of those killed during the cemetery attack, Fr Alec once again found himself
at the very centre of the drama. He recalls events as follows:

> So that day I had been told to go up to St Agnes' at the time
> the funeral would be coming out with Kevin as there would be
> somebody there from Sinn Féin and they would have a copy of
> the Sinn Féin paper for the SDLP. I went up, and was given this

paper and I was then going to go down to Derry and give it to John Hume; it was Saturday afternoon. Before that, I thought I'd go up and talk to the mother of Kevin – his family were walking just behind the coffin. I was going over towards them, I was within a yard of them when this car suddenly backed at speed through the funeral about thirty yards away to my left. This silver-coloured car suddenly backed at speed, but it got stuck because Kevin who was getting buried was a black-taxi man and therefore there was at least one, but I got the feeling that there were probably three, black taxis on either side of this funeral as a sort of guard of honour. So when the people in this car tried to back out of the funeral at speed they were stopped by the taxis … I remember one of them stood up, the man in the passenger seat … they were plain clothes, now. One of them stood up and fired a shot in the air … Then somebody, and he was obviously a republican, went over to the black taxies and he got a wheel brace and smashed the windscreen of the car and I remember thinking I'll go over and I'll talk to the driver and try and find out what's going on here … When I went back then I discovered that you had what you'd call two rugby scrums and each rugby scrum had one of the people in the car … Well, I went over to see what they were doing but they weren't kicking them or anything … So they pushed them in through the open gate, the main gate of Casement Park and put them down on their faces … And I got down between the two of them and I had my hand on each … So I was lying there on the ground and every now and then I'd shout back 'Would somebody get an ambulance' and then somebody came along and searched the top pocket of the soldier on my right and pulled out some sort of identity or pocketbook and opened it and said, 'He's a fucking Brit', and he started to kick him in the head until somebody else came from behind and pulled him away … Somebody came behind me, picked me up by the shoulders and said 'Get up or I'll fucking-well shoot you as well', and he shouted back 'Take him away' … I decided I would try to lose myself in the crowd and then come back in again … Well, I was determined that once they brought the first of these soldiers out that I was going to attack and free the soldier and get him to run like hell or something. So I was standing at the gate and the next thing I realised that, instead of bringing them out the gate, they were putting them over the wall where we had been lying ... They were letting them down this wall and there were people down below catching them and they had a black taxi ... I ran down into this side street, determined that I was going to do something when I got there and I was hoping to get there before they had finished letting down the second one, but unfortunately when I got down this black taxi had started driving away ... I had the key in the door of [my] car, when I heard two shots ... I went in and one of them seemed to be breathing and he was lying on his back and I knelt down and started giving him the kiss of life ... and then somebody came in behind me and touched me on the head or shoulder and said, 'Father, that man is dead' ... Now, under my arm – this is another poignant story in all of this – under my arm I had the Sinn Féin paper ... and the Sinn Féin man met me and he said, 'Have you still got the document after all that?' and I still had the envelope but, you see, one of the soldiers had blood on him and it got onto my hand and from my hand it got onto the envelope, and I said to him, 'I have it but there's British blood on it.'

One of the photographers at the scene of the deaths was David Cairns, whose photograph went around the world the next day. Fr Alec – who had for years been working with such discretion – found his picture on the front page of the newspapers of the world.

Contacts with Dublin

Dramatic as such events are, they do not reflect the reality of Fr Alec's day-to-day engagement in peace ministry during the years leading up to the ceasefire in 1994. And it is important to remember that we are talking about years. To have received a positive response to his letter from John Hume in 1986 was indeed a breakthrough, but it was only the beginning of a twelve-year journey towards the Good Friday Agreement.

Having opened up contact between John Hume and Gerry Adams, Fr Alec then focused his attention on links between both of these and the Dublin government. His entrée into this scene was facilitated by Irish writer and broadcaster Tim Pat Coogan, and brought him to the residence of Charles Haughey, then leader of Fianna Fáil. Haughey was wary of engaging in talks because of his experience in the gunrunning trial at the beginning of the Troubles. What Haughey did do, which was to prove absolutely vital for the peace process, was to introduce Fr Alec to Martin Mansergh, his adviser.[41] Fr Alec instantly recognised a powerful ally in the quest for peace. Recalling their first meeting at Haughey's home, Fr Alec describes the scene as follows:

> One day I remember going up to see him [Haughey] and I used to go on a Saturday for some reason. It was on a Saturday morning and he said, 'There's a man in the next room and I want you to meet him.' So I went in and was introduced to Martin Mansergh. After about five minutes I knew, I said to myself this is the right man. His manner, you know, he is a real gentleman, very respectful and I knew he understood the whole thing, that if he was dealing with somebody he would understand the whole thing. He's a great historian, he's an historian by profession. But he has a great knowledge of the republican movement, an amazing knowledge of the tradition of the IRA and the whole history of the IRA, and a perfect understanding of the modern IRA; he was a man sent by God in a way.

These immediate intuitions of Fr Alec would prove to be very accurate. Since Martin Mansergh was kept on as adviser both by Albert Reynolds and Bertie Ahern when they in turn became Taoiseach, he provided an invaluable source of continuity and political expertise. From the point of view of Fr Alec's contribution to the peace process, for many years his primary contact with the Dublin government was through Mansergh,[42] with whom he had regular meetings. In an interview for this book Martin Mansergh confirmed the importance of Fr Alec in this phase of the negotiations, particularly in terms of opening and keeping open channels of communication.

The first objective was the articulation of a common position between the three nationalist entities, the Southern government, the SDLP and Sinn Féin. Since there were no direct meetings between all three of the parties, the role of Fr Alec was vital as the intermediary who went between the parties carrying drafts, of which he himself was often a co-author.

As time went on it became clear that things were in a kind of stalemate: the Irish government was insisting that it could not enter talks without a prior cessation of violence, and the IRA was saying that it would only end violence when such talks were underway. Fr Alec was one of the key figures involved in breaking this stalemate.

An article in the *Irish Times*
In 1990 Fr Alec took the, for him, unusual step of writing an article for the *Irish Times* (published 29 November 1990). The setting was the controversy surrounding the Hume–Adams talks while violence was still going on. The article is quite long and contains a number of points that help us understand Fr Alec's role. He begins by formulating what he sees as the underlying problem in the form of a question:

> How do you apply the principles of democracy to the present conflict especially at the point where British unionists say that Northern Ireland should be united to Britain and under British jurisdiction because this is the political wish of the majority of the people who live there, namely, the people of the unionist tradition while, at the same time, Irish nationalists say that Northern Ireland should be re-united to the rest of Ireland and under Irish jurisdiction because this is the political wish of the majority of the people who live in Ireland as a whole, namely, the people of the nationalist tradition?

Fr Alec goes on to explain that proponents of each of these positions have used military force to defend it. He then states that the republican movement recognises that it also needs political methods. The key statement is that:

> I am convinced, however, that the Republican movement will not be persuaded to give up its armed strategy for a political strategy unless it has first been satisfied that such a strategy would be organised enough and strong enough to pursue effectively the broad thrust of the traditional aims of Irish nationalism in the political setting of the 1990s.

He finally acknowledges that there is a kind of impasse between the respective positions, and suggests that the Church should take the initiative in facilitating these forms of contact.

This article, written in November 1990, marks the halfway point between the involvement of John Hume in 1986 and the first IRA ceasefire in 1994. The key to breaking the deadlock was the so-called Quid Pro Quo Accord between the Irish government, the SDLP and Sinn Féin. After years of negotiations, a formulation was eventually found that was acceptable to these three parties.[43]

Before examining the significance of this accord, it is important to note another key piece of the jigsaw that was at last finding its place: the position of the loyalist paramilitaries. Here, too, Fr Alec had his part to play.

Contact with loyalist groups

As noted above, the loyalist paramilitary groups gradually became more political in the course of the 1980s. Similar to the way in which Sinn Féin had emerged as the political wing of the IRA, political parties such as the Progressive Unionist Party and Ulster Democratic Party emerged as the political wings of the Ulster Volunteer Force and the Ulster Defence Association respectively. In the early 1990s Gusty Spence, the first leader of the UVF, tried to coordinate these groupings in a forum known as the Combined Loyalist Military Command.

As we have seen, Fr Alec's contact with individual unionists and loyalists goes back to his early work in Clonard in the 1970s. He speaks of Gusty Spence as a personal friend. One amusing anecdote that Fr Alec recounted is the occasion on which he was invited to a meeting of the CLMC. When one of the commanders complained that they were receiving no responses to their enquiries from Dublin, Fr Alec brought the house down when he leaned over towards this man and softly sang 'Put your sweet lips a little closer to the phone'.[44] The fact that he was invited at all and could take such liberties is a sign of the esteem in which he was held.

Formalising the peace ministry

One of the challenges facing peace ministry in Northern Ireland was that there was no blueprint. For many years Fr Alec worked substantially alone, albeit with the approval and support of his local community and of the Redemptorist congregation. With the arrival of another Redemptorist, Fr

Gerry Reynolds, on the scene in 1983, this began to change. Even if for reasons of secrecy much of what Fr Alec did he continued to do on his own, there was a shared conviction among his confrères that the peace ministry needed to be more formalised. Over the years a range of documents was produced seeking to articulate the approach to be taken in this ministry. Later we will examine this approach more closely. It is worth anticipating two important developments. One is a response written by Fr Alec to a request on the part of Cardinal Tomás Ó Fiaich to articulate in writing the rationale of this peace ministry. This document, entitled 'Pastoral Ministry and Political Violence',[45] contains the germs of Fr Alec's later thinking and also of his retrospective thinking on the whole peace process, which he articulated on various occasions as 'Lessons From the Streets'.[46] The other important development was the involvement of future President Mary McAleese in this peace ministry in 1996. This meant that she was available as a much-appreciated support to Fr Alec during the trying times that followed the breakdown of the ceasefire.[47]

There was a phase in the early 1990s in which the ministry of Fr Alec to republicans and that of Fr Gerry Reynolds in Protestant, unionist and loyalist circles converged. One strand of these contacts involved bringing Sinn Féin into contact with Church people from the Protestant community. At the personal initiative of Fr Alec in the early 1990s, Gerry Reynolds organised meetings in Clonard. Their importance is not that they achieved anything directly but that they helped in mutual understanding.[48]

The Quid Pro Quo Accord
Only with the passing of time and with the changes in the broader political configuration did direct contact between Martin Mansergh and Sinn Féin take place. For many years Fr Alec was the conduit of communication between the parties:

> I can remember these different versions and I writing [*sic*] commentaries on the different versions ... that's what I used to do you know ... but, you see, at that time Mansergh met me he didn't meet Sinn Féin ... and they would tell me when they brought back the documents that they didn't agree with this and I would go down and tell Dublin and Dublin would say we can't accept that ... So the documents went back and forth and he

> [Mansergh] was doing the Dublin version and he insisted and was
> very shrewd ... But when hardy came to hardy and it was coming
> up to the IRA ceasefire, then there were meetings between Gerry
> Adams, Martin McGuinness ... they used to meet in Dundalk.

After the letter of Fr Alec to John Hume in 1986 there had been meetings
between John Hume and Gerry Adams, between Sinn Féin and the SDLP,[49]
between Sinn Féin and members of the Protestant tradition, between Sinn
Féin and the Dublin government. Despite all these forms of contact, the
political situation remained a stalemate. It was changed political circumstances involving the end of the Thatcher era and the arrival of Reynolds
in Dublin, along with the changes in the loyalist approach to politics, that
combined in the early 1990s to open up new possibilities. In face of the
impasse constituted by the problem of violence, the Hume–Adams talks took
on a new life. We are fortunate in having the direct testimony of Fr Gerry
Reynolds,[50] who was present at a meeting in John Hume's house during
which Hume and Adams agreed on the strategy of soliciting a statement from
both governments to the effect that the people of Ireland should be allowed
to exercise self-determination. This is recorded in Fr Alec's report as follows:

> Then here was John Hume and Gerry Adams for a time and they
> were meeting and they made statements and eventually the two
> of them decided on a strategy that they would get the Irish and
> British governments to make a joint statement that the right
> of the Irish people to self-determination would be recognised
> unconditionally, subject to the consent of the people ... and that
> when this statement was made then the IRA would stop within
> twenty-four hours and I must have spent about eighteen months
> getting the wording for this statement ... going back and forth ...
> John Hume wrote the first wording in October 1992. He sent it
> down to Dublin and they corrected it and gave it to Sinn Féin – it
> used to take them at least six weeks before they came back. They
> would come back with wording if the British and Irish govern-
> ments say that then the IRA will stop. Then the Irish government
> – it was mostly the Irish government and Sinn Féin – John Hume
> did not come into it very much – the Irish government said the
> English government won't say that – we can't go over there, we

would look stupid, they would know that we should know they couldn't say that. Then they went at the whole thing and sent it back, adapted it and sent it back and it all boiled down in the end to about two paragraphs ... We got a version which was accept-able to the Irish government, the SDLP, Sinn Féin and the IRA ... so the Irish government brought it over – Albert Reynolds was the Taoiseach and immediately he got it – he didn't let the grass grow under his feet – he rang up John Major and made an appointment to see him the next day. They were off and of course the British when they got it, they started to water it all down, then there was a row between them. Eventually, then, they got a version – the Irish government said it was substantially the same but it was not worded the same or anything like, so Sinn Féin would not accept it and the IRA would not accept it. Well, Sinn Féin would not accept it since they had changed it, but they went ahead with that version in December 1993 ... and then they did the Downing Street Declaration and then the IRA didn't stop but Sinn Féin held consultations in nearly every part of Ireland for a period of a year and I'd say in six months the IRA had decided among themselves that they would accept and go on a ceasefire.

The problem was not just one of formulation but of timing. The solution was found in an undertaking to begin public talks shortly after the announcement of a ceasefire. Our best access to Fr Alec's role in the phase immediately before the first ceasefire in 1994 is provided by himself, retro-spectively, in the submission he made to the International Body in 1995. For chronological reasons we will examine these documents in Phase III.

The ceasefire of 1994
The closing scene of this phase of the peace process is set in Fr Alec's car. After twelve long years and endless drafts, the IRA made an announcement that had been agreed with the Dublin government. In an interview for this book, Fr Alec gives us this account of the moment he heard the ceasefire statement:

It was read out by an IRA woman on the radio. I remember sitting there listening to it. I listened to it actually driving the car and it was great ... You see, when you are going through these experiences, at the time, you don't take much notice. I was happy at the time at the idea that they'd made it and it's only, sometimes, afterwards that you realise the significance of those events ... That changed everything.

As he happily listened to this announcement, Fr Alec could not have known of the difficulties that lay ahead and of the fact that he was destined to remain a key protagonist in the ongoing quest for peace.

PHASE III: FROM THE CEASEFIRE (1994) TO THE GOOD FRIDAY AGREEMENT (1998)

'In for a penny, in for a pound'

'In for a penny, in for a pound' is a phrase used by Fr Alec to refer to the need for courage in peace ministry. The four years between 1994 and 1998 were among the most intense in Fr Alec's work, and they certainly required an enormous amount of this virtue. In the period following the ceasefire the story of this peace ministry continues to be woven into the broader, complicated story of the peace process.

The political context

Within the nationalist and republican camps in Northern Ireland there were expectations that the ceasefire would lead to Sinn Féin's inclusion in political talks aimed at a definitive settlement. The more time passed without this happening, the more Sinn Féin came under pressure concerning its support of the ceasefire. After the end of the ceasefire in 1996, Gerry Adams and Martin McGuinness engaged, with the help of John Hume, in attempts to restore it through contacts with the British government and the IRA.

In the unionist and loyalist camps the ceasefire was generally viewed with suspicion. 'Decommissioning' became the key word in the vocabulary of this camp. In 1995 David Trimble – considered something of a hardliner – replaced James Molyneaux as leader of the Ulster Unionist Party. Extremely important in these years was the ongoing emergence of the political wings of paramilitary loyalist groups such as the UDA and the UVF. Other groups, such as the Loyalist Volunteer Force, persisted in paramilitary action until 1998.

In the Dublin camp, too, this period saw much activity. In a first dramatic incident, Albert Reynolds resigned in November 1994. In December 1994 John Bruton was elected as Taoiseach in a coalition with Labour and Democratic Left. Another coalition, involving Fianna Fáil and the Progressive Democrats, took over after a general election in June 1997, with Bertie Ahern as Taoiseach.

In the British camp the key change came in 1997 when Tony Blair was elected prime minister with a comfortable majority. This radically altered the political balance at Westminster, where the unionists had formerly been necessary for the survival of John Major.

In this phase of the peace process, the United States played a crucial role. The appointment of Senator George Mitchell to Northern Ireland in 1995 as Bill Clinton's economic adviser was highly significant. He was to chair first the International Body, then the talks leading to the Good Friday Agreement and later the Review Body. Bill Clinton himself visited Northern Ireland in this period, and was actively involved by telephone in the final stages of the negotiations leading to the Good Friday Agreement.

These being the main players involved, let us now briefly review the sequence of key events in which they interacted. The first of these is undoubtedly the public appearance together of Albert Reynolds, John Hume and Gerry Adams at Government Buildings in Dublin just days after the ceasefire announcement. In 1995 Northern Ireland Secretary Patrick Mayhew laid down conditions ('Washington 3') for Sinn Féin's entry to talks, which included prior decommissioning. When John Bruton took over as Taoiseach the political focus shifted to the document *Frameworks for the Future*, signed by Major and Bruton in February 1995.[51]

In January 1996 the International Body led by Mitchell suggested that decommissioning and talks should take place in parallel. On 9 February 1996 the IRA marked the end of its ceasefire with a bomb in London's Docklands. As a consequence of this, Sinn Féin was not included in the talks that began at Stormont in June 1996. On 26 August 1997 the Independent International Commission on Decommissioning was established. On 20 July 1997 the IRA renewed its ceasefire. In September 1997 Sinn Féin signed the Mitchell Principles, opening the way for inclusion in multi-party talks. Throughout this period the march at Drumcree was an annual source of tension, culminating in the death by arson of three young children in 1998. After long wrangling, the Good Friday Agreement was signed in April 1998 by representatives of most of the participants in the conflict.

The role of Fr Alec Reid

It is within this complex and constantly changing configuration of political circumstances that Fr Alec continued his work for peace. The IRA ceasefire of 1994 inevitably changed the nature of his role. After the ceasefire, governments and politicians were no longer under the same kind of pressure to refuse to talk to Sinn Féin because of continuing violence. It was precisely this lack of contact that Fr Alec had managed to breach by facilitating contacts between Sinn Féin and other parties. Now that direct contact was possible, Fr Alec was much less needed in this role. From the sources available it is apparent, however, that he was by no means inactive in this period. He was uniquely positioned to understand the position of Sinn Féin. Some of the most politically technical documents written by Fr Alec date from these years. Given the political stalemate that arose out of the dispute over decommissioning, the role of the International Body chaired by Senator George Mitchell was crucial. The best documentary access we have to the thinking of Fr Alec in this period is through his submissions to that body and through a long letter he wrote to Senator Mitchell in 1996 before the restoration of the ceasefire. Before examining these documents, it will be useful to locate them in the context of Fr Alec's memories of this period.

Fr Alec was aware of two factors of which people less familiar with Sinn Féin might not have been fully conscious. The first of these was the nature of the Quid Pro Quo Accord between the Irish government, the SDLP and Sinn Féin. As its name suggests, this accord was based on the inclusion of Sinn Féin in the pursuit of a common nationalist alternative strategy in exchange for a cessation of violence by the IRA. The very basis of the accord would be eroded if, following the ceasefire, there was no effective progress on the nationalist political front. The second was the difficulty faced by the Sinn Féin leadership – primarily Gerry Adams and Martin McGuinness – in convincing the IRA to call and keep the ceasefire.

The report of Fr Alec Reid to the International Body on Decommissioning (1995)

From a political point of view the most extraordinary text we have written by Fr Alec is probably his long submission to the International Body on Decommissioning. To understand Fr Alec's thinking, there is no substitute for reading through this text, which is available in the Documentation section of this book. What follows here is a gloss on the submission aimed at explaining how it ties into the different political circumstances outlined above.

Before getting into details of content, it is worth making some preliminary points about this submission. The first of these concerns its length. As submitted to Mitchell, with the opening letter, the text runs to over forty pages. This includes a certain amount of repetition. It is also important to recall the context. Many months had passed between the ceasefire in August 1994 and the preparation of this submission. Contrary to nationalist expectations, the British government was not moving towards organising inclusive talks, partly because of Major's position at Westminster. John Bruton's public stance on the peace process – as expressed for example in his responses to statements of British policy by John Major – tended to be less open and progressive than that of Albert Reynolds. The International Body had been convoked by the British and Irish governments with a view to discerning how to make progress on the decommissioning issue. Fr Alec's purpose in his submission was clearly to convince the commission that Sinn Féin and the IRA were in good faith but that action was needed if the ceasefire was to hold.

As well as noting this historical context, it is worth noting the very particular style of this document. It is long, indeed prolix, repetitive and technical. It is clearly the purpose of the submission that dictates this style. The purpose is to persuade the highly experienced members of the body about what needs to be done. In doing so, what Fr Alec does is effectively retell the story of the peace process (from his point of view, naturally) from 1986 onwards – that is to say, during a period of nine years. This submission gives us unique access to the earlier, largely hidden, phases of the peace process. It does so, however, not simply as historical narration but in a submission indicating how to understand the current situation and how to plan the future.

We may now examine the submission itself more closely. The covering letter helps us perceive Fr Alec's self-understanding and the logic according to which the submission is organised. In the opening sentence Fr Alec describes his role as a 'witness' to the negotiations and agreements involving the Irish government.[52] We know from what we have seen so far that his role went well beyond that of being a witness. More important are the following two paragraphs of the covering letter:

> In circumstances where I would have to act as such a witness I shall always testify in an honest, independent and forthright way. To do otherwise would be to dishonour the integrity of the Quid Pro Quo Accord and the sanctity of the nationalist commitment to the principles of democratic and peaceful politics which that Accord represents and embodies.
>
> It would also dishonour the integrity of the pastoral ministry for peace which I have been conducting for many years with the support of the Redemptorist Community at Clonard Monastery,

Belfast, and the approval of the Redemptorist Provincial Superior,
Very Rev. Brendan Callanan C.Ss.R and his predecessor, Very
Rev. Raphael Gallagher C.Ss.R.

The first paragraph helps us to understand two points that will be repeated
ad nauseam in these documents: that the Quid Pro Quo Accord is the key
to peace, and that this accord is based on the personal integrity of those
representing the parties. It is only by closely studying the documents that
the full significance of these points emerges. Extremely important here is
also the tone of the writing: 'formal but passionate' might best describe it. Fr
Alec, perhaps more than anybody else, knew what was at stake if the Quid
Pro Quo Accord were to collapse or to prove ineffective.

The second paragraph is a formal confirmation of what we have seen at
various points along the way. Fr Alec saw himself and wanted to be seen by
others, including the members of this body, as representing the Church. This
fact lends authority to his submission, and remains of tactical importance
in facilitating contacts between the parties.

The covering letter then explains the logic of the way in which the
submission is presented. It comprises four documents (Document No. 1,
Document No. 2, etc.). Given the immediacy and urgency of the decommissioning issue, this question is treated separately and at length in Document
No. 1. Document No. 2, which is much briefer, simply presents the accord
in a more formal way. Document No. 3 is the most historically interesting
in that it puts the meeting in 1994 between Reynolds, Hume and Adams
in historical perspective. Document No. 4 fills out the picture by pointing
up the position of Irish nationalists in the North as the 'test issue' of the
peace process.

It is common to read in the literature that the peace process begins in
1993. If by 'process' we mean the formal negotiations between the parties
and the governments, this view is perhaps tenable. One collateral contribution of Fr Alec's submission to the International Body is that it helps us to
appreciate how much of the work for peace was done before 1993. There
can be no doubt that Fr Alec was absolutely central to this hidden phase of
the peace process.[53]

Rather than attempt a summary of the contents of these lengthy and
sometimes repetitive documents one by one, we will now attempt to present
and comment upon the key arguments presented in them taken en masse.

- The 'armed struggle' between 1969 and 1994 must be viewed within the broader history of Irish politics, at least since the time of the French Revolution. In various other documents, and again here, Fr Alec makes the distinction between the 'armed force' tradition and the political tradition. He is unequivocal in his personal adherence to the political tradition, but is utterly committed to dialogue with those in the 'armed force' tradition. Viewed in this perspective, what is at stake in 1994 and the following years is not simply the resolution of the Troubles. What is at stake is a change in the course of Irish history.

- The precise nature of this change constitutes the second major point. As a fruit of his discussions with Gerry Adams, Fr Alec became convinced quite early on that a consensus among the nationalist people of Ireland, North and South, was the only path to peace. The documents explain in some detail why this is so. It is vital to appreciate the degree of political calculation involved here. If the Southern government, the SDLP and Sinn Féin pursued separate agendas, then the resistance and hesitation of Britain and the obdurate opposition of unionists and loyalists would prevent a peaceful resolution of the conflict. It is only in terms of this political equation that the IRA attitude to decommissioning and such issues as a time frame for negotiations can be understood. A key word in these documents is 'dynamic'. This is used in relation to an 'alternative strategy', meaning that the IRA can only be persuaded to call a cease-fire if convinced that the alternative strategy in pursuit of a settlement (which must at least allow for the possibility of a united Ireland) has a reasonable chance of succeeding. To have such a chance it must be strong enough, dynamic enough, to overcome predictable British and unionist/loyalist opposition. When both these camps actually delayed the process after the ceasefire, for the IRA and Sinn Féin this meant that the dynamic was being lost. This was enough to put the whole idea of the accord into question.

- An important part of this political calculation was its conceptual breadth. Fr Alec is at pains to point out that the idea is not to combine nationalist political forces so as to crush unionism. It is, on the contrary, to combine nationalist political forces around an objective and a method that respect equally the unionist and nationalist traditions in Ireland.[54] There is a constant appeal to justice, and more specifically to human dignity and human rights.

- A final point concerns the whole idea of psychology in these documents. Fr Alec understood republican psychology more than most people. He understood why the IRA ceasefire had been such a difficult objective. He knew what it would mean for that organisation to surrender arms. And he knew what it meant for them when their effort at peace, revising their most fundamental convictions, had been met with suspicion, duplicity and dragging of feet: 'They simply went back to war.'[55]

A letter to Senator Mitchell

As noted above, what Fr Alec feared for the ceasefire actually happened in February 1996 when the IRA set off a huge bomb in London. Given the sceptical attitudes towards the ceasefire of both the British and unionist camps, such an event was seen as confirming their worst suspicions. It also put the architects of the peace process and the ceasefire into a difficult position. They now had to convince the other parties that they and the IRA were serious about peace while bombs were exploding. The formal contacts took place through John Hume, but once again Fr Alec is at the centre of affairs, particularly with regard to contacts between Sinn Féin and the other players. One key player at this stage was once again Senator Mitchell. In November 1996 Fr Alec wrote a letter to Mitchell with a view to helping the senator understand the Sinn Féin position. As was the case with the submission to the International Body, this letter throws light on how closely Fr Alec was involved in this late phase of the peace process.

Apart from repeating some of the main background themes already treated in his earlier submission, this letter analyses in great detail the current state of affairs. There is once again the tone of gravity and urgency. Most of all there is cogent, logical, lucid argumentation aimed at persuading the senator about what needed to be done to ensure the restoration of the ceasefire.

This letter, which is considerably less prolix and technical than the submission, is also available in the Documentation section of this book. What follows is again a kind of gloss that attempts to illustrate the links between the letter and the current political circumstances. The key points made in this letter might be summarised as follows. Since June 1996 the political situation has become dangerous in that the possibility of an unequivocal restoration of the ceasefire has been placed under threat. Should the ceasefire not be restored, the possibility of civil war would loom. 'It is not, in my opinion, too much to say that the historical Irish conflict is now moving towards a climax in a context which has the potential for a peace that would be better and a war that would be worse than ever before.'

Fr Alec uses the term 'critical mass' to refer to IRA suspicions about British and unionist readiness to reach a settlement through negotiation. On this point it is vital to recall what was said earlier about the 'dynamic' envisioned after the ceasefire. This dynamic, which was the basis of the Quid Pro Quo Accord, was to take the form of a concerted effort by the nationalist camp (with its three main components, the Irish government, the SDLP and Sinn Féin) to promote peace through a just settlement. The first ceasefire, the public meeting of the three leaders at Government Buildings, and John Hume's unstinting commitment to the peace process were a first delivery on this accord.

In general, the response of the unionist groupings had been predictably obstructive. Most disturbing was what seemed to be changes in the British position and, to a lesser extent, in that of the Irish government. This is the political context in which such candid statements as the following are to be read: 'To reduce the Government input on the issue to a policy of encouraging the participants to agree among themselves on a time frame and calendar would, in Sinn Féin's view, be a recipe for inefficiency, filibustering and ultimate failure because it would not move the Unionist parties to co-operate.' This last point is the reason why Fr Alec in this letter identifies the time-frame question as the 'acid test' of British intentions. 'The acid test in that proposal is their suggestion for a timeframe because, in effect, it is also their suggestion for a dynamic which would have the capacity to focus the peace negotiations and to move them forward in an efficient way towards a negotiated settlement.'

It is highly significant that in this letter Fr Alec puts much more emphasis on this than on the other two IRA conditions: the admittance of Sinn Féin to talks, and 'confidence-building' measures that would reassure the nationalist community. The reactions to the first ceasefire had in fact shown that a ceasefire of itself is not enough to bring about peace. It must be followed by genuine efforts of all parties to reach a definitive settlement. The reactions of the unionists and the British to the first ceasefire left Sinn Féin, and with them Fr Alec, acutely aware of the need to integrate the ceasefire into an effective political dynamic.

We have no way of knowing exactly how these considerations weighed with Senator Mitchell and his colleagues. What we do know is that in 1996 the International Body suggested that talks and decommissioning should occur together. The least that we can say is that, not for the first time, there was a happy convergence between the opinions forcibly expressed by Fr Alec in his various documents and letters and the indications given by the august senator.

PHASE IV: 'THE DISAPPEARED' AND DECOMMISSIONING, 1998–2005

'Keep on keeping on'

'Keep on keeping on' is a phrase used by Fr Alec to refer to the need for perseverance in the face of obstacles during peace ministry. He had already practised this virtue to an impressive degree in the long years leading up to the Good Friday Agreement. When his help was needed on some specific questions after 1998, he typically 'kept on keeping on'.

Depending on how one understands the term 'peace process', it can be understood as ending in 1998, in 2007 or as still ongoing. Good arguments can be made in favour of each of these, and maybe of other possibilities. Whatever about of all that, there is little doubt that Fr Alec's contribution to the peace process was substantially complete by the time of the Good Friday Agreement. In the years between 1998 and 2005 he remained involved in peace ministry in Northern Ireland in two different ways, partly at the request of republicans. One of these was in acting as mediator between the IRA and the families of the 'disappeared', the other was as witness to IRA decommissioning. Before examining the form of this involvement more closely, it will again be useful to set the political scene.

The political context

The period immediately after the Good Friday Agreement was marked by political wrangling between the parties, which went on for years. The results of the referendums in May 1998 already gave eloquent expression to the problem: in the South there was overwhelming support; in the North there was majority support but substantial opposition among unionists and loyalists. This made the position of Official Unionist leader David Trimble very difficult. The major point of contention was decommissioning, which had been on the political agenda since the IRA ceasefire of 1994. Senator George Mitchell was called back to Northern Ireland in 1999 to chair a review of the implementation of the Good Friday Agreement. Trimble eventually agreed to enter a power-sharing Executive with Sinn Féin prior to any decommissioning but in the expectation that this would follow. In February 2000, in the face of very slow movement on decommissioning, the secretary of state, Peter Mandelson, suspended the Executive. The June 2001 Westminster election saw a strengthening of the position of both Sinn Féin and Ian Paisley's DUP. This trend was to continue and increase in elections in the following years. In a gradual and staggered process, the IRA first declared that decommissioning had begun, then permitted control of some dumps, and, finally, after the terrorist attacks in the United States in September 2001, engaged in effective decommissioning. In 2005 the Independent International Commission on Decommissioning announced that all IRA arms had been put beyond use. As regards the issue of the disappeared, soon after the Good Friday Agreement the British and Irish governments set up the Independent Commission for the Location of Victims' Remains, with corresponding legislation, to facilitate the recovery of the remains.

The disappeared

In the years following the Good Friday Agreement the role of Fr Alec in peace ministry changed dramatically. No longer bound to silence, he gave a number of interviews, including acclaimed television programmes such as the BBC's *14 Days* and RTE's *Would You Believe: The Secret Peacemaker*. He also continued formulating his reflections on peace ministry in documents that we will examine in the second part of this book. He received various awards for peace, one of which involved travelling to Yale University. No longer needed as a conduit between the parties in Northern Ireland, he was invited to fulfil a similar role in the Basque conflict, which meant spending a lot of time out of Ireland. So we can talk in general terms of him moving away from the whole Northern scene during these years. Against this trend, soon after the Good Friday Agreement, and at the request of the IRA, he became involved in the question of the disappeared.

The 'disappeared' are those killed during the Troubles, mostly by the IRA, whose remains were never recovered. Although some of these deaths date back to the 1970s, it was only after the Good Friday Agreement that the question came to prominence in the public eye. This was due in part to a statement by the IRA in 1999 to the effect that it intended to facilitate the location of the remains of the disappeared. It is at this point that Fr Alec becomes involved. We do not have written reflections on this ministry from his hand, but he made a poignant statement in an interview:

> I would like to mention also the families of the 'disappeared'.
> Those who never had the bodies of their loved ones returned to

them to enable the grieving process to properly take place; one of the hardest crosses to bear, one of the most painful experiences anyone could have. May the Lord comfort and support them.

These words were born of extensive contact with the families of the disappeared in the years following the Good Friday Agreement. We are fortunate to have direct testimony of this ministry by Fr Brendan Callanan, the provincial of the Dublin Province of the Redemptorists at the time. Asked on different occasions about Fr Alec's role with regard to the disappeared, Fr Callanan made the following statements:

> About Easter 1999 the IRA stated that it would reveal the place of burial of the nine disappeared people so that the families could hold a funeral service. Fr Alec was invited to contact each of the families and to liaise with the authorities, especially in Dublin, because the graves were located in the Republic. I accompanied him in this work. After Easter we visited each of the families a number of times to explain the process and to listen to what they had to say. Naturally this was a very traumatic time for the families and that was another reason we made regular visits to each of them ...

> Towards the end of May we were brought to the various sites, seven in number, and took some notes so that we would know how to return with the representative of the ICVLR [Independent Commission for the Location of Victims' Remains] who as it transpired was Eamonn Mulligan. As soon as we got the information from the republican representative we made an appointment with Eamonn and brought him to the seven sites and gave him all the information that we had received regarding the location of the graves. There was one site in County Wicklow and two each in Counties Louth, Monaghan and Meath. It was Eamonn's task to contact the garda officials and they would be the ones to carry out the searches ...

The searches began towards the end of May 1999. One body was found on the first day of the search, another two about three weeks later. A couple of years later two more bodies were located. At various times over the years the search was suspended and then taken up again with the help of more sophisticated equipment. At the time of writing, four of the original nine have not yet been located.

In the light of organised campaigns by different groups representing the families, the whole issue became quite a political 'hot potato' in these years. The interest of the two Redemptorists involved was essentially pastoral, as Fr Callanan concludes:

> Throughout the period of the searches we continued to visit the families, not least because we had a pastoral obligation towards them. Contact with the families was maintained after the suspension of the searches.

When Fr Alec definitively left Belfast, his role with regard to the families was taken over by another Redemptorist confrère, Fr Paul Turley.

Decommissioning

Paradoxically, the final stage of Fr Alec's involvement in the peace process is in some ways to be attributed to Ian Paisley. After one of the reports of the Independent International Commission on Decommissioning, Paisley had declared his distrust of John de Chastelain and demanded that two clergymen oversee the acts of decommissioning. The names that eventually emerged were Harold Good, former Methodist president, and Alec Reid. Even though, over the years, both had been involved in creating links between loyalist and republican paramilitaries, it was only during this phase that the two men got to know and appreciate each other. Fr Alec recalls the actual decommissioning operation with some pathos:

> It was a three-storey house and they were obviously republicans ... and it must have been five or six times we stayed there ... We came down every morning at half six and this van arrived, it was all boarded up ... Well, this man used to arrive. He was quite young but he was a member of the IRA army council, there are seven ... So we'd go off at half six every morning and we'd sit into the back of this van ... So when they had put all their weapons beyond use, while this was happening there was one of the IRA people walking up and down with a rifle ... And we were standing there when Rev. Harold Good pointed out to me 'Just

watch this' … he went over to the General de Chastelain and he handed over the rifle, it was the last gun you know.

Part of the brief of the two independent witnesses was to report to the political parties. This meant that Fr Alec had occasion to meet personally with unionist leaders, including Ian Paisley. His memories of this occasion are worth quoting extensively as a scene that, in different ways, symbolically illustrates and celebrates the work of a lifetime:

> As regards Mr Paisley, when we had witnessed the decommissioning Harold and myself had to go to all the political parties to tell them that we had witnessed the decommissioning; without telling them how, but assuring them, on our word of honour, that it had happened … one of my memories of talking to the unionists … now this would have been the Ulster Unionist Party … There were five of them and I remember sitting there talking and reassuring them about this and feeling very much at home with them and feeling almost one of them. I remember saying to myself, God, I feel towards these people as if they were nationalists. It was an interesting experience, to feel that you were at one with unionists … So then we went to see Mr Paisley, we went to the DUP office at Stormont and Harold Good was with me, but I went in first, anyway, and Mr Paisley was sitting in a big armchair and he came over and he shook hands with me and said, 'You are very welcome, Alec', and then he went over and sat down in this big armchair … Now, Harold Good was sitting alongside me and Mr Paisley was over there and Harold had his foot on my foot the whole time, my left foot, in case … I'd say something, so the whole time we were there he had his foot on mine and he would press it if I would start … you know, and what happened was he wouldn't let me talk and I remember saying to myself, to hell, he's cutting me out here, and after he explained to Paisley all about the decommissioning, he started to waffle to prevent me talking, and I said, to hell, I'm going to get in here, but Paisley noticed that I was having trouble getting in and he said to me: 'Do you know, Harold Good is a Methodist and there's one thing you don't understand and that is when a Methodist starts to talk

you can't stop him.' I don't think Paisley could see our feet ...
and I did talk, I made a point of saying what I wanted to say to
Mr Paisley ... and I spoke for about forty minutes or more and
I remember thinking to myself afterwards, he's a good politician
because he sat there and he listened and he never interrupted us,
all the time we were talking, he just sat there and listened.

The question of decommissioning, which had bedevilled the peace process
for over ten years, was gradually put aside with the decommissioning of
loyalist weapons in the following years. It is surely most appropriate that
the 'one-man peace process' who had set out to convince the IRA to stop
in the 1980s should have been so actively involved in these decisive closing
moments.

Part one conclusion
In accordance with the logical arrangement of this book, thus far we have
attempted to narrate the story of this peace ministry in an historical perspective. Before adopting other perspectives, in order to gain a more complete
picture it will be useful to draw some provisional conclusions based on these
four phases of the story taken together.

Our examination of the different phases confirms the idea expressed
earlier that we are dealing here with a story within a story. The decades we
have examined witnessed the presence and influence of many individuals and
groups on the political scene in Northern Ireland, London and Dublin. Fr
Alec is thus one of many protagonists in a very complicated story. What seems
reasonable to conclude is that he was the primary initiator of the efforts at
peace that eventually led to the Good Friday Agreement in 1998. Stimulated
by his own pastoral experience and inspired by the political vision of Gerry
Adams, at a certain point Fr Alec took initiatives of decisive importance.

Primary among these initiatives was opening up and maintaining contact
and communication between the different components of the nationalist
'cause'. As time went by, this peace ministry required widening the range of
contacts so as to include all the main players nationally and internationally.
Of considerable importance during these contacts was the written word.
For many years the negotiations between the different parties took place
through the exchange of written documents. Fr Alec was absolutely key in
the formulation, delivery and exchange of these written texts.

As we read through these different phases it is important to remember that we are viewing matters in hindsight. In this perspective the story has a (fairly) happy ending: we have (relative) peace. We must remember that as Fr Alec and companions were living through these events they did not have this consolation. On the contrary, failure after failure, bomb after bomb, death after death meant that the prospect of peace was very dim indeed.

Another significant point that emerges from the narration is that this peace ministry came to birth slowly and painfully. The very word 'process' is quite misleading, especially in the first decade of the conflict, because it suggests a planned, organised undertaking. The reality was much more hit and miss, trial and error. What eventually comes to be articulated as a pastoral plan for peace ministry is the fruit of lessons learned and experience accumulated over long, trying years.

A final point evident in the different phases is the complexity of Fr Alec's enigmatic personality. He was a man of many faces and many voices depending on what was needed at a given moment. The warm, friendly face of the pastor is in contrast with the sharp, penetrating look of the political mentor. The soft, kind voice we hear in the television interviews contrasts with the rigour and cogent argumentative force of some of his written texts. Add to all this that both by nature and by necessity Fr Alec was often taciturn, and we can begin to appreciate how difficult is was for others, including his own confrères, to really get a hold on who he was. And yet the extraordinary fact is that over the years this quiet, reserved individual developed pastoral contacts of different kinds with many categories of people: the local Catholic people, the local Protestant community, the republican prisoners and their families, loyalist paramilitaries, the IRA, government officials from Belfast, Dublin, London and the United States, Church leaders … There is something paradoxical about the fact that such a retiring personality found himself increasingly cast in a prominent, public role.

Given these circumstances we can legitimately conclude that one of the defining features of Fr Alec was his extraordinary tenacity. What has been told here in quite a brief space actually occurred over decades. The emotional impact of seeing so much suffering and the psychological frustration of not being able to change things was an enormous burden. It is only by more fully understanding the resources Fr Alec found in faith, the subject of the second part of this book, that we can begin to understand how such a huge commitment was possible.

PART TWO
Reflecting in Faith

Peace ministry as lived Gospel

When Christian believers hear the word 'Gospel' they may well tend to think immediately of what they hear being read at the Sunday liturgy. Or they may think of written texts such as the Gospel of Mark or the Gospel of John. Less immediately, they may understand by 'Gospel' what Jesus of Nazareth actually preached in the concrete circumstances of his day. Or, indeed, they might think of the living person of Jesus Christ as the Gospel. All these ways of understanding 'Gospel' are legitimate, and all are related to each other in various, rich, mysterious ways.

In the second part of this book we will consider yet another sense in which we can understand 'Gospel'. We will call this 'lived Gospel', meaning the life of a specific Christian when that life itself becomes a proclamation of the Gospel. In our case the specific Christian in question is Fr Alec Reid, and our task now is to consider in what sense his peace ministry can be perceived and understood in this way. Another way of saying this is to consider how the actions and words of Fr Alec were in effect another way of doing what Jesus Christ did and said, or another way of proclaiming what the Gospel of Mark proclaims.

How can we go about establishing that this is so? By examining, in faith, what Fr Alec said and did? Certainly so, but let us not forget various factors that render our access to this ministry difficult: it is, especially at the beginning, a secret ministry about which Fr Alec deliberately did not talk. It often took the form of editing and re-editing complicated political texts in which there is little or no mention of Christian faith. It took years and years for Fr Alec to understand and articulate his own role, and the whole context of this ministry is marked with blood and tears that often obscure and overwhelm efforts at peace ministry. The claim that this ministry is an example of lived Gospel must take account of all these complicating circumstances. Given all this, we are most fortunate to have the text of a lecture delivered by Fr Alec Reid in 1993 in St Clement's Retreat House, Belfast, entitled 'The Role of the Servant of Christ in a Situation of Political Conflict'.[56] This text can serve as a kind of window through which we can gain access to Fr Alec's peace ministry as lived Gospel. Clearly, we must read the text in the light of the historical account of the peace ministry that we have already narrated, for it was there that the Gospel was lived/proclaimed before Fr Alec prepared this lecture. What follows then is a reflection in faith on the historical account by means of a commentary on the lecture. The purpose of the commentary is to help the reader to perceive better a dimension of this peace ministry that does not come out fully in the historical narrative, namely the way in which this ministry is based on faith in the Gospel of Christ. It is hoped that text and commentary together will amply illustrate that what we are dealing with here is indeed a powerful, contemporary proclamation of the Gospel.

The role of texts in Christian ministry

From the beginning, texts and Christian ministry have gone hand in hand. This is so if we take 'the beginning' to be the narration of the Genesis story, the letters of Paul to the first Christian communities, or the composition of the Gospels. In order to better appreciate the major role played by texts in the peace ministry of Fr Alec it is worth reflecting briefly on this idea in more general terms.

Let us consider, as a kind of illustrative parallel, the ministry of St Paul to the Christian community at Rome, as this finds expression in the Letter to the Romans. We know that Paul writes this letter almost thirty years after the death of Jesus Christ. As a Christian and an apostle, Paul interprets the life, death and Resurrection of Jesus Christ in and through faith. The members of the community at Rome are people who believe in the risen Christ. Paul understands himself as a servant of Christ in the service of such communities. As such, he addresses a letter to them in preparation for a visit. The writing and sending of this letter is in itself an act of ministry with a view to future ministry in the community. So when we pick up the Letter to the Romans, we are involved, whether we realise it or not, in a mesh of relationships between a text, a form of ministry and people of Christian faith.

What has all of this to do with Fr Alec in Belfast in the 1980s? Not very much, perhaps, if one is content to remain in an historical perspective. If, however, our intent is to understand the significance of this peace ministry in terms of Christian faith, then the example of Paul's ministry is enlightening on a number of scores. In fact, Fr Alec's ministry, just like Paul's, is simply not intelligible without reference to the life, death and Resurrection of Jesus Christ. Not intelligible, that is, as ministry. It is of course possible to study the political significance of this ministry in an historical perspective, as we have attempted to do, but this is not yet to understand it as ministry. To understand this ministry as ministry, we must think of it as Fr Alec does, that is to say as the work of a servant of Christ who is continuing Christ's mission of salvation.

A second instructive parallel concerns the relationship of the two authors to contemporary faith communities. Fr Alec, like Paul, understands himself as a servant of Christ in the service of Christian communities. Like Paul, he uses texts as an instrument of ministry. His texts do not take the form of pastoral letters, at least not in the same sense as those of Paul, but they are texts that he produces in the course of his peace ministry, and are thus, for us, an extremely important point of access to that ministry.

A third instructive parallel concerns the relationship between texts and later faith communities who share in the same faith tradition. Just as we Christians today can read profitably Paul's letter to the Christian community at Rome, so, too, we can read the texts that Fr Alec produced in service of the Christian communities to which he was ministering in Northern Ireland. So that when we take up 'The Role of the Servant of Christ in a Situation of Political Conflict', written by Fr Alec more than twenty years ago, we are also involved in a complex set of relationships between a text, a form of ministry and people of Christian faith.

The Role of the Servant of Christ in a Situation of Political Conflict

Introduction

Before taking up our commentary on the different sections of the text, some more general introductory comments will help set the context. The first of these concerns the relationship between this text and the peace ministry of Fr Alec Reid. This peace ministry, as we saw in the historical narrative, was an incredibly long, complicated and trying business. The full story, what we might call the 'lived history', of what Fr Alec and his companions did will never be told. What we have in our historical narrative is a much reduced account of what actually happened day by day and night by night during long, hard years. The text we are about to study can help fill out this story in various ways. Written in 1993, it can best be understood as sharing the distilled wisdom accumulated by Fr Alec in almost twenty years of peace ministry. We must appreciate at the outset that the text is not a narration of this ministry but an explanation of it in terms of faith. We the readers, on the basis of what we know about what happened historically, must try to discern the significance of what is being said here about peace ministry. We will only be able to discern the significance of it all in faith terms if we read the text with faith. It is important to allow the faith of the author as expressed in the words of the text to resonate with our faith as we have received it in the course of our lives. (The reader may recognise a process which is the daily bread of anyone who reads the scriptures with faith.)

A second introductory comment concerns the genre of this text. Formally a lecture, it is perhaps better understood as a kind of apologia for, or justificatory explanation of, this peace ministry. There are also good grounds for considering it a kind of 'mission statement', as we would say today, in that it identifies pastoral objectives and indicates strategies. It is important to remember that there was no blueprint for peace ministry in this context: all the participants, including Fr Alec and his immediate confrères, such as Fr Gerry Reynolds, had to slowly articulate their self-understanding of this ministry. Throughout the 1970s and into the 1980s, the degree of alienation in Northern Ireland mounted with the rising level of violence. From the point of view of ministry, this posed a problem for Church officials. Many priests and bishops saw their pastoral duty as being that of condemning the violence and invoked basic Christian moral principles as the basis of this condemnation. There were a number of problems with such an approach: it was ineffective in that the violence continued; it did not propose, or contribute to, concrete alternatives; it was not based on real knowledge of the 'men of violence'. The mission statement we find articulated in this brief document is an effort to articulate a different ministerial response to the political conflict.

A third introductory comment concerns the relationship between this text and the many, many other texts written by Fr Alec. Most of these are 'reports' or 'commentaries' on political discussions and negotiations between the parties. Their style is correspondingly dry, technical and slow moving. Our text, by contrast, is brief, fresh, lucid and eloquent. It is also one of the few texts in which Fr Alec meditates explicitly in faith on this peace ministry. These factors make this text the most appropriate one for trying to understand the significance of this ministry in terms of faith, but it must be remembered that what Fr Alec is talking about here was actually being put into practice as he wrote the other texts. So the best way to understand his peace ministry would seem to be to comment on this text in the light of other available texts and the events to which they refer.

A final introductory comment concerns the way the lecture is structured. It divides neatly into three sections dealing respectively with the vocation of the servant of Christ in conflict, the basis in scripture for this ministry, and practical indications about how the ministry should be organised. Our commentary will follow this ordering, but will insert references to various related themes and documents as seems appropriate.

First section: the vocation of the servant of Christ

The very first sentence of the text makes an important statement about the role of the servant of Christ, namely that he or she must be 'in the midst of conflict'. Elsewhere in this text, and in many other places, Fr Alec insists on this 'hands-on' approach to peace ministry. The reason why this form of contact is necessary is explained as follows:

> Serving Christians must stand in the midst of conflict and encounter it in all its flesh-and-blood reality until they come to understand it with the knowledge of personal experience. This is the only kind of knowledge that will enable them to identify the

moral dimensions of good and evil which are involved in causing
the conflict.

If we read this statement in the light of what was said above about the
response of the Church to violence, it already contains the key elements
distinguishing this approach to ministry from those current at the time.
Rather than condemning acts of violence ineffectually from a distance, the
servant of Christ is called to go towards the conflict, understand its causes,
get to know the participants, and actively promote a just solution. The difference between the two approaches is not that one is concerned with the
immorality of violence and the other is not, but rather that the approach
of condemning violence at a distance is seen as being pastorally, and indeed
morally, inadequate. Precisely in order to be able to make an adequate moral
response to the conflict, the minister must be in the midst of it. It is crucial
to note at the same time that the minister is not called to be morally neutral
but rather 'to discern all the moral issues to which the conflict gives rise
and then to take up a position on each of them'. An important word in
this statement is 'all'. The great criticism levelled against the institutional
Church in these decades by many nationalists and republicans was that the
condemnations of violence did not include all forms of violence being used
by all those involved. A key to Fr Alec's peace ministry is that it involves the
views and experience of all participants in a serious, direct, personal way.

The theological and scriptural inspiration of this approach will be discussed below, but elements of this are anticipated in the opening section of
the text when Fr Alec takes up the theme of surviving as a peace minister.
To go towards conflict and expose oneself to it is a very demanding form
of pastoral engagement. To endure the kind of risk, frustration, rejection,
disappointment, depression and even despair that inevitably accompany this
kind of commitment is even more demanding. Again and again, Fr Alec
insists that there is only one way to survive as a minister of peace: by total
dependence on God:

> I believe that Christians will not survive, let alone succeed, unless
> they are inspired by the conviction that the Holy Spirit is always
> present and that they are sustained by the enabling power that
> flows from that conviction.

This kind of communion with the Holy Spirit brings gifts such as under-standing, wisdom, prudence, courage, patient endurance and compassionate love. Sensitive to the needfulness of the peace minister, Fr Alec insists that only with God's help will it be possible to persevere, 'to keep on keeping on'.

What echoes of the Gospel can we hear in this first section of the text? We may begin with the very idea of a 'servant of Christ', a term which immediately resonates with the opening words of St Paul's Letter to the Romans ('Paul, a servant of Jesus Christ, called to be an apostle, set apart for the gospel of God ...') as well as with the servant theme in the Hebrew scrip-tures. As with Paul, this term expresses Fr Alec's self-understanding. We saw in the historical account that everything Fr Alec Reid did, he did consciously and explicitly as a priest and Redemptorist. This text helps us to appreciate that even more fundamentally all that he did, he did as a servant of Christ.

It is significant that the reference to Christ is immediately followed by a reference to the Holy Spirit. While quite capable of bantering with Gerry Adams about the Holy Spirit as a kind of code for talking about how things were going politically, this and many other texts remind us that in Fr Alec's life the Holy Spirit was anything but a frivolous matter. For him it is only in the power of the Holy Spirit that the servant of Christ can serve. This is a truth Fr Alec had lived for many years before articulating it here as part of this mission statement. The years of unstinting faithfulness to the mission give his words authority – another idea that rings bells with those who know the Gospels.

In order to appreciate more fully the key relationship between what Fr Alec says in this text and what he had been doing in the previous decades of ministry, the idea of 'inscription' might help. In its common usage, 'inscrip-tion' means carving meaningful signs into stone, for example. In a figurative sense, this idea is sometimes used to talk about the way in which human beings 'write themselves' onto the world or into life. This idea applies not only to 'historical figures' but to all of us. Through our words and actions we leave traces of our passing, most of all in the individuals and groups we meet. There can be no doubt that this is true in a dramatic way of Fr Alec during the peace process (as we saw in Part One). At this point, however, we are faced with a highly significant fact: Fr Alec inscribed himself not just in the events of the world, but also in many, many texts. Of these many texts, the one in which he most eloquently inscribed himself as a person of faith is the one we are commenting upon. It is a marvellous grace for us to have a text in which so much lived faith finds verbal expression: this opens up the possibility of gaining access to the faith that was the source of this ministry through a careful reading of this text.

If this is so, we must interpret Fr Alec's ministry not just as his work but also as the work of the Holy Spirit in him. Apart from his explicit, opening declaration that this is so in the ministry of the servant of Christ, we find many other indications that it is so in this text. For instance, the 'compassionate love' mentioned in this section and referred to later in the text as 'compassionate companionship' must be understood in relation to the real, lived, compassionate love that Fr Alec brought to hundreds and hundreds of suffering people in his ministry. Remembering the historical events, or reading this text, we come across traces left by Fr Alec. For Christians, these traces need to be interpreted not just as historically significant events but also as historically significant events in which the Spirit of God was moving. Inspired by the Spirit, Fr Alec acted and spoke in ways that gave expression to that Spirit, that is to say, in ways which proclaimed the Gospel.

One word that comes to mind reading this section of the text while keeping in mind preceding historical events is the word 'dynamic'. As we saw in the historical account, at a certain point Fr Alec was moved to 'do something' about this conflict. In this text he is insisting on constant interaction with the Spirit of God. So there is a fascinating link between the faith dynamic and the political dynamic, between pastoral initiative and political initiative. The form of faith described in this text changed the course of Irish history, or at least significantly contributed to doing so. Only those who lived in Belfast day after day, month after month, year after year, listening to the grim tale of violence and revenge can fully appreciate how difficult it was to believe that this violence could be stopped. Fr Alec's faith in Christ, in the power of the Spirit, and in the compassionate love of God gave him a different view of this seemingly hopeless situation. Faith in God here translates very concretely and even pragmatically into faith in political processes and faith in the people who can make them work. It is rare in contemporary, fragmentary, secularised culture that Christian faith and realpolitik come so close to each other with such beneficent consequences.

Second section: scriptural guidelines

Having considered the role of the Holy Spirit in the vocation of peace ministry in the first section of this text, Fr Alec moves on in the second section to articulate some 'scriptural guidelines' for this work. It is important to keep in the mind the context in which these guidelines were formulated. Most of all it is vital to remember that no blueprint was available to Fr Alec and his companions as they wrestled with the question of what to do as servants of Christ in such a conflict. In a certain sense the Gospel itself serves as the blueprint for this ministry. But let us not forget the political reality in which Fr Alec was operating and had been operating since returning to Belfast in the early 1980s. The standard position was that no dialogue was possible with Sinn Féin until the IRA stopped the violence. Convinced of the inadequacy of such a stance, for years Fr Alec and others stood in the midst of the conflict and asked themselves what the servant of Christ should do. We have seen in the historical narrative what they decided upon and to what effect. What we have in the second section of this text is Fr Alec's explanation of how sacred scripture inspired and guided this discernment. So let us attempt to understand the significance of a text written in 1993 for a form of ministry that had already been going on for at least ten years.

Looking to the ministry of Jesus as depicted in the Gospels for inspiration and guidance, Fr Alec immediately focuses in once again on the need to be in the midst of conflict in order to respond to it. As on many occasions, he invokes here the theological idea of incarnation to explain the approach of Jesus:

> How did Jesus accomplish his role as the agent of God in the conflict situation that is human life? By living in the midst of it until he became bone of its bone and flesh of its flesh ... He allowed himself to get caught up in all its dimensions of good and evil, from the level of the individual to the level of those who wielded political and religious power, but always as the agent of God's justice and compassion.

Read with faith, this brief text invites commentary on a number of different fronts. Not to be overlooked is the almost throwaway phrase 'the conflict situation that is human life'. Fr Alec is not talking here about the conflict in Northern Ireland but the conflict that is human life *tout court*. Such an affirmation is not unproblematic because it could be confused with the position of someone like Thomas Hobbes, who depicts the world as constitutively conflictual and then draws certain political conclusions. The affirmation is also problematic because it does not distinguish between the conflict that is human life as such and those particular forms of conflict that sometimes arise because of collective political divisions and animosities. These are just some of many complex 'open questions' to which the ministry of Fr Alec gives rise in political, ethical and philosophical terms. This is not the place to go into these questions, but it will be no harm to notice them *en passant*.

For our immediate purposes we can safely assume Fr Alec's purpose here is not to propagate liberal political theory but simply to note that conflict was an important element in the life of Jesus, as it so often is in human life. His question then becomes: what did Jesus do about such conflict? What he absolutely did not do was keep his distance and moralistically denounce those involved. What he did do was go towards the conflict and expose himself to the risks involved 'as the agent of God's justice and compassion'. We are here at the core of the Gospel. We are actually dealing again with the role of the servant of Christ, but doing so now with a focus on scripture. This affords us a marvellous opportunity. What Fr Alec says about Jesus in scripture helps us to understand how he conceived of his peace ministry, following this blueprint so to speak. But, read in faith, the inverse process is also possible: what we know of Fr Alec's ministry can help us to understand the ministry of Jesus. It can do so, certainly, because it is so much closer to us culturally and historically. More profoundly it can do so because it is a continuation of the ministry of Jesus.

Moving on from this bedrock conviction, Fr Alec goes on to spell out the form that the ministry of Jesus took on. The key idea here is that of 'companionship', meaning the way in which Jesus is often depicted in the Gospels at table with people, sharing food and drink while developing understanding and friendship. Scandalously, in the eyes of many, this offer of companionship is not limited to the 'politically correct':

> Jesus was prepared to share his company with anybody who was prepared to share his or her company with him, no matter how good, bad or indifferent their relationships with God and their fellow men and women might be.

Statements such as this could be extracted from many post-Vatican II commentaries on sacred scripture. What makes this text by Fr Alec signifi-cant in a faith perspective is the glaring link between it and what he had been engaged in for over a decade. Here again the text and the ministry are mutually revealing: following the example of Jesus, Fr Alec chose to offer companionship to those involved in conflict before the conflict was resolved – indeed, with a view to trying to resolve it. On the other hand, if we imagine the kind of hysterical attacks made on those who engaged in the peace process because they were talking to those associated with violence, we can understand, or rediscover, the way many righteous people reacted to Jesus. For us today the figure of 'prostitutes and sinners' has become a bit pale and innocuous because so often used, with the consequence that it no longer causes real scandal. If we replace it with 'terrorists and paramilitary organisations' we might be much closer to grasping a disturbing but central dimension of the Gospel.

There are two other related points in this section on scriptural guidelines that warrant comment. The first is expressed as follows:

> To those who accused and even rejected him for associating with the wrong kind of people, Jesus gave various replies, including those in the parable of the Pharisee and the Publican (Lk 18:11), with all its implications for not being judgmental about anybody whose personal conscience before God cannot be fully known.

The other, which concludes this section, runs as follows:

> If the Christian does not seek to engage in dialogue and companionship with all the participants, he or she will not be able to address all the moral issues to be resolved.

The first of these statements refers directly to the experience and message of Jesus as depicted in the Gospels; the second makes the link to the theme of peace ministry in political conflict. Both together constitute the core of Fr Alec's apologia for a form of peace ministry that was characterised by taking the initiative towards those involved in the conflict. All those involved. What is stated here in principle, and justified by appeal to the practice of Jesus, we know to have been lived out in the midst of terrible tensions over a period of twenty years. Looking back from the relative comfort of today, it is not always easy to understand how this approach provoked such visceral negative reaction.

Third section: a pastoral strategy

The final section of the text is very different in character from the first two, but can only be properly understood in association with them. It attempts to draw out the practical consequences of these background truths by articulating a concrete pastoral strategy for situations of conflict. Empowered by the Spirit of God and inspired by the example of Jesus, those who wish to engage in peace ministry must decide what is to be done. As a bridge between the second and the third sections, we find the following statement:

> Based on these principles, a strategy for addressing the conflict in Northern Ireland is suggested here. It is essentially a ministry of communication, characterised by the Spirit of Christian dialogue.

The brief phrase 'a ministry of communication' in this statement warrants some comment. We must read this phrase in context: violence was rampant at the time and Sinn Féin was excluded from communication. From Sinn Féin's point of view the 'armed struggle' was considered legitimate precisely because ordinary political resolution was not possible. This stalemate went on in different forms for years and years, with more people dying all the time. The phrase 'a ministry of communication' is a very accurate and succinct way of expressing what Fr Alec and his companions did. They saw their ministry – that is, their task as servants of Christ – as that of opening up communication between the parties. There are at least three lessons here that may be all too easily overlooked. One is that when communication breaks down between human beings, we can expect trouble. This domestic truth can be applied to communication between groups and communities. This is what had happened in Northern Ireland in a dramatic way and is at the root of the Troubles. Another lesson is that the only way to peace is to establish or restore communication, for to persist in not listening to the other parties is to ensure that the conflict will continue. This, too, is precisely what happened for decades in Northern Ireland. The third truth, maybe not quite so obvious, is that a believer wanting to serve Christ in such circumstances should see the task of establishing or restoring communication as ministry: this is the key way to make God's presence effective in these circumstances.

These basic truths are spelt out in the next paragraph, which leads to the articulation of the first practical steps to be taken. This paragraph repeats in synthesis what had been said in the earlier sections about making direct contact with all involved, but adds this important phrase: 'with a view to deciding a Christian pastoral response to each of them'. The Christian minister, therefore, is called upon not just to offer 'compassionate companionship' but also to actively seek out a solution. It is this pragmatic aspect of peace ministry that requires the articulation of a pastoral strategy, as outlined in a first set of three steps:

- The first step would be to list all the participants in the conflict and to grade them according to their significance for its resolution.
- The second step would be to meet authoritative representatives of all the participants with a view to explaining the role of the Christian ministry to the conflict and to persuading them to cooperate with it.
- The third step would be to set up a programme for pursuing the strategy of the ministry in an organised, dynamic and, therefore, effective way.

Rereading the three steps listed here, we must again try to understand them in their historical and pastoral context, otherwise they might seem too easy. The first step speaks of *all* the participants. All the participants in the Northern Ireland conflict by the time we get to 1993 means a lot of people, some of whom would understandably inspire fear and doubt in the most zealous peace minister. The second step involves meeting the leaders of all groups. This is key to Fr Alec's ministry: his political judgement left him in no doubt that he had to go to the top people on all sides. At this point a fascinating question arises for those of us who read this text years later: is what we see outlined here a programme for the future or a description of the past? The answer would seem to be that it is both. There is no doubt that by 1993 Fr Alec had personally done, and not just once or twice, all the things listed in this text, so there is description going on. At the same time the first ceasefire has not yet been called and there are indications at the end of this section that Fr Alec felt the need for a team peace ministry, so there is also an element of planning.

The third step in the response acknowledges the need for direct, constant, organised contact with the participants. The quality of this contact is spelled out in another paragraph:

Whenever and wherever within this conflict, the serving Christian hears the word of truth, the word of justice, the word of compassion, he is hearing the words of Jesus and listening to his message for the resolution of this conflict. This is another way of saying that where truth is, where justice is, where compassion is, Jesus is. Where love is, God is.

Such a horizon considerably shapes the way in which the minister listens to the parties. It revolutionises the understanding he or she has of the conflict, and is the key to being able to invite, with sincerity and conviction, all the parties to become involved in dialogue. It is just the opposite of a facile response that sees all or most of the blame for the conflict in one of the parties. It is not difficult to imagine the difference this attitude makes from the point of view of the person being listened to. It is precisely the patient, caring acknowledgement of the truth and justice within my position that might make it possible for me eventually to recognise the absence of such truth and justice in some other aspects of it. Having made this step for myself, I am much more likely to be able to see and understand the truth and justice within the position of my adversary, as well as the lack thereof in other aspects.

This third step finds effective realisation in a second set of four steps that constitute the following phase of the strategy:

- Identify the elements of moral truth and justice in the party position that has been explained, and then set them out in writing with reasons for accepting them as such.
- Identify any elements in the position explained that would not be compatible with the principles of moral truth and justice, and then set them out in writing with the reasons for not accepting them.
- Give the representatives of the party concerned a written response to their explanation of their party's position with a view to developing the dialogue with them. This response would set out the points of agreement and the points of disagreement between the Christian pastoral position and the party position. The dialogue would then concentrate on the points of disagreement with a view to sorting them out and reaching more and more agreement between the two positions.
- Inform each and all of the parties to the conflict of the elements of moral truth and justice that the Christian reconciliation ministry had

discerned and which it would support in the political positions of the other parties, and then ask for an authoritative response to this information from each party.

There is something of a contrast between the lofty, visionary language of the earlier sections of the text and these pragmatic passages. If the essential lines of the former can be drawn more or less directly from scripture, the inspiration of this later section is not so obvious. The pragmatic, programmatic style can blind us to the profound theological vision underpinning this strategy. By taking this section paragraph by paragraph, it should be possible to understand more fully how faith and pragmatic pastoral practice are combined here as they were combined in Fr Alec's peace ministry.

The horizon within which this strategy is articulated is that of faith in salvation and the implications of that faith for the practical affairs of life, particularly where there is conflict. When conflict is viewed without faith, it can lead to attitudes such as resignation, scepticism, cynicism or despair. Such attitudes, while understandable as emotional reactions to particular circumstances, cannot constitute the Christian response to conflict. This must take salvation seriously and go in search of the concrete form that it can take on in given circumstances. It is this conviction of the peace minister that makes listening to, and dialogue with, the protagonists of violence possible, and promises to make them fruitful. The key assumption of the Christian minister in dialogue with those involved in conflict has to be that there is some legitimate claim to truth and justice in the position of each party. The first task of the servant of Christ is to acknowledge, attend to and venerate this truth and justice.

The fascinating thing is the way in which the text conceives of Christian ministry as a kind of catalyst making this kind of growing understanding possible. The image used in the text for this growing understanding is typically that of common ground:

> It [dialogue] also helps to uncover and identify the common moral ground between all the parties to the conflict – the only ground where agreement and reconciliation can be established.

We find in this statement another example of one of Fr Alec's favourite metaphors: that of sanctuary or sacred space.

An interesting detail is worth noticing. One of the key strategies proposed for identifying this ground is that of the written word. The position of each party is written up, it receives a written response from the peace-ministry team, the party is invited to reformulate its response in writing, it receives in writing the positions of other parties, and responds to them in writing. We are again here dealing both with memories and projects at the same time. What we here see laid out as a programme we know from our historical account to have been a key activity in Fr Alec's ministry for years and years. At the same time it is a key part of the pastoral strategy being proposed here for the future. Long, hard experience had clearly taught Fr Alec that human beings in conflict will better grasp truth and justice if they see them in writing.

What can we conclude about this peace ministry on the basis of our reading of this key text? The most important conclusion, which is echoed in many other texts, is undoubtedly that peace ministry is based on faith in the Gospel. This faith provides both the inspiration and the enabling power that make the ministry possible. The main practical consequence of faith in a time of conflict is readiness to place oneself within the conflict at the side of those involved. Compassionate companionship is the foundation upon which dialogue with the participants is built. This dialogue must be based on the sincere conviction that each of the parties is moved by some legitimate vision of truth and justice. The service of peace ministry is to affirm these elements while patiently challenging elements not compatible with truth and justice. Having done this with the parties, peace ministry attempts to do it between the parties by pursuing with them the common ground upon which they can agree. It is here and only here that peace can be restored.

Part two conclusion

Having completed this commentary on the remarkable text we have been examining, it is now time to return, by way of conclusion, to the idea with which we began this essay. In the light of all that has been said above, how might we formulate an interpretation of this peace ministry as lived Gospel? This claim might be more fully articulated as follows:

- The peace ministry of Fr Alec constitutes a contemporary incarnation of Jesus Christ, a graced moment in the history of salvation.
- As such, it also constitutes a moment of revelation in which we can more fully grasp the mystery of salvation in Christ.

- The whole story can be the occasion of further grace through the response of Christians to this revelation.

Let us briefly elaborate on each of these points. It is standard Christian doctrine that the Spirit of God comes to dwell in believers, particularly through faith, prayer, sacred scripture and the sacraments. Christ is incarnate in his Body, the believing community. Our claim here is that this common truth finds vivid and special expression in the peace ministry of Fr Alec. As he himself was fond of doing, we cannot overemphasise the 'corporeal' nature of this ministry: we are talking about Christ present in the body of Fr Alec or in the body who was Fr Alec as he went about his ministry. The most striking icon we have of this truth is the famous photograph of Fr Alec Reid with the dying corporals: a Catholic priest with pronounced republican tendencies risking his life in an attempt to rescue and bring solace to the suffering of those who represented the other side in a bloody political conflict. Is this not a radiant manifestation of God-with-us?

This brings us to the claim about revelation. While Christians believe that God has definitively revealed God in Jesus Christ, they are also aware that their capacity to perceive and adhere to Christ in faith is not closed. Just as we remain open to receive new and deeper illumination every time the Word of God is preached or read, so, too, we must be open to the Word of God in historical events. It is our claim that in the events narrated in this book, the believing Christian can perceive anew the glory of Christ. While certainly respecting the obvious differences in degree, it might well be said of Fr Alec what is so truly said of Jesus Christ: this is what the mystery of God looks like when lived out in human form.

Another basic truth of Christian doctrine is that God reveals God not for our information but for our salvation. This implies that the revelation is only fully effective when it wins the response in faith of the believer, in Christian community and as an individual. Applying this general truth to our particular case, a disturbing truth dawns: God's glorious revelation of God in the peace ministry of Fr Alec is not fully complete without our response.

PART THREE
Testimonials

Funeral service reflections by
Ruth Paterson, Mary McAleese,
Harold Good and Michael Kelleher

Personal reflections on the life of Fr Alec Reid by
Gerry Adams, Brendan Callanan,
Martin Mansergh, Ken Newell, Derek Poole,
Martin McGuinness and Gerry Reynolds

THE LESSON OF FR ALEC'S LIFE

Reflection offered by Rev. Dr Ruth Patterson at the ecumenical service for Fr Alec Reid at Clonard church, Belfast, 26 November 2013

During the last few days there have been thousands of words used as many different people have sought to express their thoughts and feelings on hearing of the death of our dear friend and pilgrim for peace, Fr Alec Reid. Tonight I have been asked to reflect on the lesson of his life. There are others who are far more qualified than I to comment on the effectiveness of his huge contribution to our peace process. My only qualification is that we were gifted with a friendship which I deeply valued.

Like anyone who finds themselves on a road less travelled, his journey was a lonely one. And for him, Restoration Ministries, my community, was a safe place where he could drop in unannounced and simply be himself. For someone who had promises to keep and miles to go 'before he slept', to be able to make a phone call from any number of unnamed destinations and just talk was, I think, for him a gift and certainly for me a huge privilege.

I cannot separate Alec the man from Alec the priest and Alec the peace-maker. He was his vocation – and the Spirit of the Lord was upon him, holding these three roles together in one person. He had feet of clay, like the rest of us, but, with deep humility, allowed himself to be seized by vision. It was not so much he who had chosen such a course but rather, to paraphrase a one-time secretary general of the United Nations, Dag Hammarskjöld, the way that had chosen him and he must be thankful.

Archbishop Desmond Tutu once described himself as a prisoner of hope. Alec was similarly convicted. He never, ever gave up. One of the biggest challenges during the Troubles was to simply keep on keeping on trusting that there would be an end, a good outcome. For such a frail-looking man, often plagued by illness, he had huge tenacity.

A word used very often in the New Testament is endurance. Alec had that in abundance. At the funeral of Martin Luther King, the president emeritus of Morehouse College where King had been a student said: 'He was not ahead of his time. Every man is within his star, each in his time. Each man must respond to the call of God in his lifetime and not in somebody else's time.' Then he listed, like a roll call of faith, those who, throughout the centuries, had to act in their lifetime. 'None of these,' he says, 'were ahead of their time. With them the time was always right to do that which was right and that which needs to be done.'

Alec followed the star that had risen for him and remained true to the light that had fallen into his heart, not only for a way out of our conflict, but also for so many who were and are victims of those hard years, including the families of the disappeared. His commitment to peace was not confined to Ireland, as we know, but was global, most notably in the Basque region in Spain. Like a bridge over the troubled waters of violence, loss and anguish, he laid himself down. It was his time and it was the right time. The Spirit of the Lord was upon him.

Beatitude person

For me, and many others, Alec was a beatitude person. If you break the word down it simply means, 'Let this be your attitude'. First and foremost, he was a citizen of that upside-down kingdom whose hallmarks are mercy, humility, purity of heart, a hunger for justice, peacemaking and a willingness to pay the price to see right prevail. Ray Davey of Corrymeela used to say to us, 'Jesus never ever said, "Blessed are the peace lovers." He said, "Blessed are the peacemakers."' This world has far too many armchair pundits for peace, but too few of those who are willing as 'children of God' to embark on such a messy and costly journey. With eyes wide open, Alec set out on such a path. Why? For him there was no option. The Spirit of the Lord was upon him.

Sheila Cassidy, in her book *Good Friday People*, speaks of those like Alec who travel this way: 'As they walk they will, each in their own good time, arrive at their kairos moment, the point of choice, of decision, of a stiffening of the sinews because danger is in the air and there is no going back.' His attitude was shaped by his citizenship and inevitably he had an effect on the world around him.

Beyond his public persona, Alec had the maturity of someone who knows who they are and has moved beyond the either/or and the labelling, judgmental response that can characterise so much of our living. He knew who he was. He did not refuse to let his actions be determined by the label others put upon him, nor did he categorise or box the other. What he always saw was another human being in desperate need of help. Within him there was a huge well of tenderness. Patrick Mathias says that tenderness 'involves compassion, the capacity to suffer with the other person with the vision of a shared future'. If this is not too strange a comment to make, I think Alec already lived, in the now, that shared future because he had been grasped by the vision of peace and unity. The Spirit of the Lord was upon him.

Love of Church universal

He had a love for the Church universal but was not blind to its shortcomings. He was able to say some hard things without being destructive. In many of our conversations he used to say to me, 'Ruth, when this is all over (this meaning the Troubles) you and I will have to sort out Mother Church!' He was also a strong advocate for greater involvement of women in Church and state, being totally convinced that had there been more women in key positions of influence, the conflict that affected all of our lives for so long would have been resolved much sooner.

In recent months Pope Francis has delighted Catholic and non-Catholic alike by his bias for the poor, by calling for a culture of encounter, making space for honest dialogue, a daring to enter into complex webs of relationships, a recognition that this is a kairos time to show mercy, an acknowledgement that the feminine genius is needed wherever there are important decisions to be made – and much else. In all of this Alec was truly his brother. The Spirit of the Lord was upon him.

Central to the belief system of the small and struggling Algerian Church is what they call the sacrament of encounter as they try to understand how a tiny Christian community can manifest the love of Jesus in an overwhelmingly Moslem culture and environment. They have been seized by the ethical urgency of encounter. It is the call to enter into relationship with the other, a relationship that becomes a source of life for both.

Fr Christophe Theobald says, 'Each time that conscience and relationships overcome violence, each time that a link is made and strengthened by means of a significant encounter, and that sometimes at the price of someone's life, the Spirit of holiness is at work.' Alec lived the sacrament of encounter and there is a sense in which he paid the price with his life. To truly encounter the other is sacramental, and, for Christ's ones, it is not an option. It is a command that comes to us from God himself. If we are truly living it, it will always be in the shape of a cross. And it need not involve words – sometimes it's better if the words are few but the commitment is unmistakable. It was unmistakable in Fr Alec Reid. The Spirit of the Lord was upon him.

FELLOW TRAVELLER

Reflection offered by Rev. Harold Good at the funeral Mass of Fr Alec Reid at Clonard church, Belfast, 27 November 2013

It is often said of someone who has made a unique contribution that when history is written that person will be given his or her rightful place. Happily, in the case of Fr Alec Reid, neither he nor we had to wait until after his death for a rightful acknowledgement of his contribution to the process, which has brought us to where we now are.

For me it is a very special privilege to be asked to share a personal tribute to my very good friend and brother in Christ.

Fr Alex and I may have appeared to come from very different directions, as indeed we did. Geographically, he was a Tipp man while I a Derry man. Churchwise, we came from two different denominations. But we soon discovered, and took delight in, what we had in common. We were not too far apart in age; we enjoyed the same sort of humour and banter. And we shared a love of travel. Travelling with Alex was always an adventure!

Ironically, the best known of our shared journeys was a highly secret one. Like a couple of Old Testament patriarchs, we set out not knowing where we were going or, more correctly, where we were being taken. But, for Alex, that journey was to be a culmination of all that he had longed for, prayed for and worked for. I shall not forget that moment when he whispered in my ear, 'There goes the last gun out of Irish politics.' What a moment, for him, and for all of us!

That journey was one of many we were to share across these islands and across the seas. And on those journeys I soon discovered that Fr Alex possessed two essential gifts for good travelling. The first was the gift of instant friendship. When welcomed aboard by a flight attendant, for example, a typical conversation would go like this: 'And what is your name, dear?' 'Marie Therese.' 'Marie Therese! What a beautiful name. I've always loved that name ...' and/or 'I have a sister (or an aunt, or a cousin) by that name.' I was always fascinated by the number of relatives with the appropriate name. But whatever we had paid for, from then on we would be treated as 'business class'! It was a wonderful gift which he used to such good effect on his journeys into unknown political territory and to build trust with and between strangers.

The second was his ability to fall asleep and wake up upon arrival! In a way this was how he coped with situations and conversations which he felt to be irrelevant or pointless.

But Alex and I were fellow travellers on what for us was the most important journey of all – our journey of faith, two fellow pilgrims often stumbling, seeking to follow in the footsteps of Jesus; the same Jesus who had called each of us to follow him and who, when we were not much more than schoolboys, had called us into ministry, a ministry of reconciliation, in which each of us rejoiced.

This is not to say that Fr Alex and I were not aware of the historic doctrinal differences between the two traditions from which we came. Of course, we were. One could not grow up in any part of this island without being aware of those differences. But for Fr Alex and for me, difference was not about division, fear, bitterness, hatred or bigotry. We had simply been born into and lovingly nurtured in two traditions within the Christian family, two traditions from which each of us brought something which enriched the faith of the other. We were like two fellow travellers with their packed lunches, each of whom had brought food to share with the other.

Interestingly, as a study of Church history reminds us, this should not be so surprising, for historically Redemptorists and Methodists have much in common.

Both of our movements were founded in the mid-eighteenth century, one founded by Alphonsus Ligouri, the other by John Wesley, both of whom shared a passion for social justice and the practical application of the Gospel. So, in the tradition of the founders of our respective orders, Fr Alex and I discovered that we brought this same passion to our shared journey. For us, a passion for peace with justice; for an end to bigotry and bitterness that invades and destroys the human soul; for the sanctity of each and every human life; for an end to violence; for the healing of our land; and a passion for a Christ-centred solution to our conflict wherever it existed.

So, I have to confess, on our shared journey of faith, Fr Alex and I did not spend precious time and energy debating academic, theological issues. Neither of us was particularly interested in the number of angels one could dance on the head of a pin! For us, the pivotal question has been: 'In the harsh reality of our broken, divided world, what does it mean for us to live in obedience to the mind and will and purpose of the Christ who has called us to follow him?'

Of course, as so many of us discovered, these journeys were not always easy. There were many twists and turns, diversions, obstacles and roadblocks. Inevitably, there were those who did their best to discourage and divert us. At times it was a lonely journey, at others a weary one. But for Fr Alex in such moments, his standard response was, 'Leave it to the Holy Spirit.' To which I would often respond, 'Be careful, Alex, don't push him!' But how right he was, for he knew we had to wait on God's timing.

Now, this earthly part of Alex's journey has come to an end, but, for him, an even greater journey has just begun. And so, on behalf of all of us who have been his fellow travellers, I bid him an ancient blessing:

> Go forth good friend upon your journey from this world
> In the name of the Father who created you;
> In the name of the Son who has redeemed you;
> In the name of the Spirit who has sanctified you;
> And all the people of God,
> Aided by angels and archangels
> And the whole company of Heaven.

And may your journey from us bring you to a place of real and lasting peace, a peace you so richly deserve. Amen.

The Power of Love

Reflection offered by the then President Mary McAleese at the funeral Mass of Fr Alec Reid at Clonard church, Belfast, 27 November 2013

Over two hundred years ago in his famous hymn, William Cowper wrote that, 'God moves in a mysterious way his wonders to perform.' It is hard to believe Cowper wrote that without having met Alec Reid. The hymn is based on the words of Isaiah 55:8–9: 'For my thoughts are not your thoughts, neither are your ways my ways, saith the Lord. For as the heavens are higher than the earth, so are my ways higher than your ways, and my thoughts than your thoughts.'

Alec, known to some as Al, Alex, Alexander or just plain Fr Reid, may at times have seemed like an enigma, a puzzling or inexplicable occurrence – but he was far from it. He was a priest. Not a liturgy-and-lace man but a humble and ever faithful servant of Jesus; a man who really bought deeply into the idea of the healing power of love, who saw all human beings as sons and daughters of the one Father, and members of the one human family.

This was and remains utterly radical thinking in a community divided against itself by a toxic history which we did not create but which we too often recreated. In this world of people barricaded against one another by contempt, fear and hatred, battling against one another in a conflict that lasted too long and cost too much in wasted human life, there seemed precious little space for a culture of Christian love to flourish, for we Christians had mostly decided to love only our own and to remain estranged from those who were not our very own.

Into this tightly bound world of vanities, where people refused to talk to other people because of a long list of becauses, where violence sharpened tongues and hardened hearts, there came the rather quiet and humble figure of Fr Al Reid. He saw spaces for hope to grow where others saw impregnable irredentist citadels. He saw ways to soften hearts, he found words to persuade the estranged to talk to one another, to take a chance on one another, to find common ground. He believed we were better than we had become, dragged down by the dead weight of an ignoble history. He believed we could between us construct an alternative strategy that would allow us all to live humanly and decently in peace and good neighbourliness, our identities intact, our political ambitions reconciled, our future no longer soured by the poisonous spores cast by the past.

Alec believed that when no one else did, when it all seemed hopeless and he seemed daft, as he toggled between people and groups that over their dead bodies would ever talk to one another. And as he trundled his badly typed alternate strategy day in and day out year after bitter year, he never lost faith in God or hope in us. It took a dire toll on his health, as those of us who were close to him know only too well, but he never complained and the work never stopped.

Even when his quiet, prayerful, pastoral care of the embryonic peace had been of seminal help in the construction of historic ceasefires and the Good Friday Agreement itself, Alec kept on working in the service of peace, in the service of Christ and the great commandment to love one another. Invited by the Church to help if he could, in his latter years he quietly brought his distinctive genius to bear on the Basque problem, living often in great discomfort and under stresses we cannot imagine with an ailing body that needed to be cared for but which he refused to put before his work as priest, pastor, peacemaker supreme.

I remember the day of the Madrid bombing. Alec was in our house when the news came that suggested, wrongly as it happened, that ETA might have broken their ceasefire. He physically crumbled in front of me in pure distress. Just as he had done on the phone to me the day of the Canary Wharf bombing. I saw then what he so often tried to cover up, the dreadful personal toll that the needless and unconscionable taking of human life took on him. His work on those days lay in ruins. His faith in humanity was sorely tested, but not his faith in God, for always in those moments Al would reach for the same words: By the grace of God ... with the help of the Holy Spirit ... by the power of prayer.

Al talked a lot about the Holy Spirit and almost invariably in sporting terms. As you might expect of a Tipperary man, the images were of the Holy Spirit togged out in the Tipp colours wielding a hurl and him centre forward on the best Tipp team ever. For over twenty years Al would land regularly to our house. I would ask him how he thought things were. The Holy Spirit is on the subs bench, he would say, or worse still, the Holy Spirit was after getting an unmerciful clatter and was carted off the field wounded. Ominously, he would say he was going to miss a few matches. On a really bad day, Alec, a tad impatient, would say the Holy Spirit had missed the team bus. On a rare good day, the Holy Spirit was playing a blinder. He was dominating the midfield and had holes punched in the net with his miraculous goals. Al described them with passion as if he had watched them live in Croke Park. Alec patiently but relentlessly punched holes in our thinking. He let light in where we were content to sit in darkness. He skilfully set up the goals that others scored, against the odds, against the run of play. In unlikely back rooms he helped coach key members of the underdog cross-community team that no one rated, and, by the mysterious ways of the Lord, it became the team that was to score the great goal of peace. Now with the well-designed custom-made tools that are the Good Friday and the St Andrews Agreements, as John Hewitt says, we build to fill the centuries arrears.

It will take a lot of hands to fill that mighty gap, and thankfully today there are many hands doing the work. But once not so very long ago, there were just a few and among them a humble, simple priest and pastor who looked in the faces of all he met and saw not just Catholic or Protestant, loyalist or republican, but brothers and sisters in Christ, children of the one God, children made in the image and likeness of God, men and women capable of making peace, sustaining peace and living together in peace, by the grace of God.

May Alec himself now rest in his own richly deserved and hard-earned heavenly peace.

SERVANT OF CHRIST IN A SITUATION OF CONFLICT

Homily preached by the then provincial superior, Fr Michael Kelleher, at the funeral liturgy of Fr Alec Reid, Marianella, Dublin, 25 November 2013

Alexander Reid was born at Leonard's Corner on the South Circular Road, here in Dublin on the 5th August 1931 – he was a Dub. He was called after his grandfather Alexander, who converted to Catholicism in order to marry his grandmother Margaret. Alec's father died when Alec was six, Alec's sister Maura was four and the twins, Margaret and Eddie, were two years old. After his father David died, Alec's mother Dolly brought her four children back to her own family home in Nenagh in County Tipperary, where Dolly later married Jack Glennon, her sister Peggy's widower. Alec's stepfather Jack died of cancer in the 1950s; his mother Dolly died in 1981, and his brother Eddie died in 1986.

Here with us today we have Alec's sister Maura, her husband Don and their family. We also have Alec's sister Margaret, her husband Jim and their family. Fr Alec's Aunt Ita, Jack's sister, is also with us this morning; she was like Fr Alec's 'big sister' over many years.

The young Reids grew up in Nenagh, Alec attending the local primary school and later the Christian Brothers Secondary School. From an early age Fr Alec played hurling, and while a student at the Christian Brothers he captained the team. He also played for Éire Óg Hurling Club in Nenagh. In 1949 Tipp won the All-Ireland Minor Hurling Championship, beating Kilkenny 6–5 to 2–4; Alec was a panel member. He said later:

> Hurling taught you how to win and how to lose. You learned failure and how to handle it. You learned how to deal with people, how to work with people, your teammates; and how to respect the opposite side. Much later in life, if things were going badly with any of the negotiations between the various parties in the North, I would say 'Well, we will have to put the Holy Spirit in goal', and if things were going well, the Holy Spirit was a centre forward.

In 1949 Alec joined the Congregation of the Most Holy Redeemer, the Redemptorists, in Cluain Mhuire, Galway, and spent three years at University College, Galway. He took his first vows as a Redemptorist in 1950 and was ordained in September 1957 by the bishop of Galway, Dr Michael Browne.

In 1959, after completing his studies, Fr Reid began his life as a Redemptorist missionary. In 1961 he was appointed to the Redemptorist community at Clonard Monastery in Belfast, and he was based there until the late 1990s, when he moved to the Redemptorist community in Dublin.

From the start of the Troubles in the North of Ireland, Fr Alec was part of the Clonard community, which sits on the peace line. Clonard Monastery had always been a place of refuge for people, especially for suffering people. Fr Alec was always in demand by the people of Clonard and the wider west-Belfast area. He worked for many years with groups of Travellers with his great friend Anne Fitzmaurice. Day and night people were looking for him – as individuals and as families. So much so, that there were times when people had to be told he simply wasn't available. The community had to 'protect' him – as much for his own sake as for anything else. His availability took a terrible toll on him: so often he missed meals; he was often out half the night. He was more than anything else a man 'for' and 'with' people in their pain and in their need. This extraordinary availability to people in their day-to-day need and suffering is what characterised him for his colleagues as a true Redemptorist.

However, the Troubles brought new challenges. The first person to be killed in August 1969 was killed in the street behind Clonard. Clonard Peace Ministry began; its mission was to provide a *tearmann*, or sanctuary setting; Fr Alec's ministry went hand in hand with Fr Gerry Reynolds's Ecumenical Ministry. When he was asked, as he often was, who he represented in under-taking his role, Fr Alec would simply say that he represented the next person who was going to be killed or hurt in the conflict.

Fr Reid's work in the peace process in Northern Ireland has been widely recognised. His work was long term and for many years behind the scenes. Among the key actions that Fr Reid undertook was the arranging of a series of meetings between Sinn Féin president Gerry Adams and SDLP leader John Hume.

There's a funny story from those early talks. One of the earliest meetings was in the convent beside St Clement's Retreat Centre on the Antrim Road, in Belfast. Sr Eileen was preparing the room for Fr Alec, Mr Hume and Mr

Adams. She splashed holy water copiously on the chairs and put miraculous medals under the cushions … I'm not sure if any of the three men noticed the dampness or the medals … but Sr Eileen's prayers and the prayers of many others were eventually answered.

Fr Reid also acted at different times as contact person with the Irish and British governments. He played a key role in a series of events which led to the signing of the Good Friday Agreement in 1998. Later on, Fr Reid used the experience he gained from his work in Ireland to try and promote the bringing about of peace in the Basque country. He helped the families of the disappeared. And along with former Methodist president Rev. Harold Good, here with us today, Fr Reid was a witness to the decommissioning of IRA arms in 2005.

On his eightieth Birthday in 2011, Fr Alec became critically ill. He spent three months in hospital before returning to Queen of Peace Nursing Home here in Rathgar, where since then he has lived very happily and well cared for. Over the past few months his health deteriorated and he spent three different periods in three different hospitals. He died peacefully in his sleep last Friday morning with one of our colleagues, Fr Clement Mac Manuis, at his bedside.

God bless. God bless you. If Fr Alec were here this morning that's what he'd be saying to people. Fr Alec was a man of God. It is impossible to really understand Fr Alec's life and work without taking God and Fr Alec's faith in God into account. Fr Alec saw himself as a servant of Christ in a situation of conflict. For Fr Alec all those who are baptised are called and sent to be servants of Christ. In situations of conflict, all baptised men and women are called and sent by God to engage with that situation of conflict in a Christlike way.

For Fr Alec, the primary role of the servant of Christ in a situation of conflict is to be the pastoral agent of the Holy Spirit in the midst of the conflict.

The first thing to highlight is 'in the midst of the conflict'. The Christian must know the conflict 'from within' rather than 'from without'.

The crucial role for the Christian is to help in identifying the human, moral and spiritual questions, especially the moral questions of good and evil which are involved in causing and driving the conflict, then in trying to answer those in accordance with the Spirit of Christ, as Christ himself would, no matter what the personal or community consequences may be.

The serving Christian could not survive such a mission or, much less, accomplish it without the Holy Spirit and the power which the Holy Spirit alone can give us. In the first reading this morning, we heard St Paul outline how we, as individuals and as communities, have been endowed with the Holy Spirit; gifts, for example, like understanding, wisdom, prudence, courage, patient endurance and, especially, the gift of compassionate love which are all crucial to the role of the serving Christian in a situation of conflict.

The Christian is sustained by confidence in the Spirit's enabling power. This assures him or her that, however great or even impossible the adversity faced may appear to be, there is always a way through, always a way out, always a way forward which will be found once he or she waits on the Spirit's guidance and relies on the Spirit's saving power. A relationship of personal trust in the Holy Spirit is, therefore, central to the role of the serving Christian in a situation of conflict.

For Fr Alec Jesus was the model peacemaker. Jesus lived in the midst of human conflict until he became bone of its bone and flesh of its flesh. He allowed himself to get completely caught up in all its dimensions of good and evil, from the level of the individual to the level of those who wielded political and religious power. As a result Jesus became embroiled and, in the end, fell victim to the violence, both moral and physical, which is endemic to so many situations of human conflict.

Jesus used companionship as a means of exercising his pastoral influence and leadership. The word 'companion' derives from two Latin words which mean 'one who eats bread with another'; Jesus often used the table of food and fellowship as an ideal setting for explaining and, indeed, symbolising his message. The companionship practised by Jesus was of an all-inclusive nature. Jesus was companion to all kinds of sinners. He was accused and rejected for associating with the wrong kind of people.

For Fr Alec, the passage I read earlier from St John's Gospel was central to his understanding of peacemaking: 'The Word was made flesh and lived amongst us.' (Jn 1:14). For Fr Alec this was and is the crucial scriptural guideline for the serving Christian in a situation of conflict. He or she must, like Jesus, become personally involved in its full flesh-and-blood humanity until he or she knows it by heart in all its reality.

Fr Alec saw himself as doing that: as becoming personally involved in the conflict's full flesh-and-blood humanity until he knew it by heart in all its reality. The picture of Fr Alec with the two corporals is an example of that. He literally has blood on his face from giving the 'kiss of life' to one of the two men.

Following the example of Jesus, Alec had as a central strategy to create compassionate companionship with all the participants in the midst of the conflict by engaging in direct, ongoing communication and dialogue with them. The aim was to identify the moral and spiritual dimensions of their various positions with a view to deciding on a Christian pastoral response to each of them. For him the first and crucial activity was to listen – to listen in a spirit of Christian compassion and discernment to the viewpoint of the party with which the ministry was in dialogue.

Fr Alec always had a thing about people's names and made a point of using a person's name when talking with him or her. In this simple but important gesture he acknowledged and respected the dignity of that person. For Alec, respect for the dignity of each human person was a crucial attitude.

For Fr Alec, listening was and is crucial to the process of resolving a political conflict because it is by listening to the conflict itself that one discovers the formula for peace. The crucial scriptural guideline in a situation of conflict is: 'The Word was made flesh and lived amongst us.' In other words, the way to peace is to be found within the conflict itself. His experience was that it can always be found there provided those who are seeking it listen to the conflict in a spirit of Christian compassion and discernment. Just listen to the conflict in a spirit of Christian compassion and discernment and you will begin to find the words of peace taking flesh.

Within a conflict, whenever and wherever the serving Christian, with the help of the Holy Spirit, hears the word of truth, the word of justice, the word of compassion, he or she is hearing the words of Jesus. He or she is listening in effect to the message of Jesus for the resolution of the conflict.

Fr Alec's ministry of Christian reconciliation in the North of Ireland also involved his co-working with other men and women, clergy and lay people, from different Christian traditions, filled with the gifts of the Holy Spirit, who had the time, the skills, the experience and, especially, the stamina for such a demanding mission. Fr Alec had a deep conviction about the need for women to be equal partners in any human process, especially processes of conflict resolution. This conviction, which he often stressed, was felt very deeply by him, and was most likely arrived at through the deep friendship, courage and wisdom he was gifted with by the women in his life – some of whom are here! He often said to me that the Northern conflict could have been resolved much more quickly if there were more women involved!

There are several images of Fr Alec that will remain with me forever. One of them is of Fr Alec giving the thumbs up to Queen Elizabeth during the state banquet in Dublin Castle. A couple of months ago I was in Rome and I saw a postcard of Pope Francis giving the thumbs up. I bought a copy for Fr Alec and told him on my return that Pope Francis had given him the thumbs up. He got a hearty laugh out of that. Over the past few years we have had some hearty laughs together. The little postcard was in Fr Alec's bedroom in St Vincent's when he died, and the undertakers put it in the coffin with his remains. I saw it there and smiled. I pray and am confident that Jesus, the Redeemer, the Supreme Peacemaker, the Word made Flesh, will have given Fr Alec the thumbs up last Friday as he arrived in Heaven.

Alec was a good companion; he was a fond friend and had good friends. We will miss our Redemptorist colleague and friend. We will miss his courage, his vision and his remarkable modesty. And we will be proud of him always. *Ar dheis Dé go raibh a anam dílis*. Amen.

THE *SAGART*

Gerry Adams

Clonard is a place of pilgrimage. They came in their thousands this week to say a final goodbye to a good priest, a close friend, a gentle and kind-hearted man, and as courageous and humble a human being as you could ever hope to meet.

Fr Alec Reid died in his sleep in the early hours of last Friday morning. I had been with him the previous Thursday and he was in good form. Talkative, funny and enjoying his hospital tea in St Vincent's in Dublin. But his condition deteriorated. I was phoned on Thursday night and told that he only had days. I arranged to travel down on Friday to visit him but shortly after 9 a.m. on Friday morning we got word that he had quietly passed in his sleep.

I was deeply shocked and saddened at his death. For forty years I have known him as a good friend to me and my family, and a selfless and unstinting worker in the search for justice and peace. In the midst of hard times Fr Reid was always there offering comfort and solidarity and advice.

He was one of the good guys. His death is a huge loss to all the people of Ireland, to his fellow priests in the Redemptorist community, and to his family, especially his sisters Margaret and Maura, his Aunt Ita, his wider family circle and his many friends.

I first met Fr Alec in the cages of Long Kesh, where I was interned, in the mid-1970s. He and Fr Des Wilson were pioneers of peacemaking in those difficult times. Both men were deeply committed to living the Gospel message and to making it relevant to the particular circumstances in which they ministered. They developed dialogue with loyalists and facilitated meetings between us and some prominent people from loyalist paramilitarism. Both were tenacious peacemakers.

I met him again on Easter Sunday after my release in 1976, when at my request he and Fr Des – who thankfully is still with us – intervened to negotiate an end to the inter-republican feuds in Belfast. They succeeded in establishing an arbitration-and-mediation process between the different republican organisations.

Fr Alec had more freedom than most priests because he belonged to an order – the Congregation of the Most Holy Redeemer, popularly known as the Redemptorists – which fully supported the work he was doing. The Redemptorist mission is to 'preach the values and the blessings of the Christian Gospel to people everywhere but particularly to the poor, the marginalised and the downtrodden'.

The *Sagart* was ordained in 1957 and was appointed to Clonard Monastery several years later. From 1969 and throughout the intervening years of conflict, Fr Reid was constantly involved in a number of special peacemaking ministries. The objective of these was to give comfort and support to the people living at the coal face of the violence; helping prisoners and their families; and promoting understanding and reconciliation between the people of Belfast. He was also chaplain to, and worked closely with, the Traveller community in Belfast.

Another Clonard ministry was to foster dialogue and friendship between the separated Christians of Belfast, an enterprise he took especially to heart, working tirelessly to move the conflict off the streets and onto the conference table.

Fr Alec was also a friend of the prisoners and part of the line of communication between them and the British government during the first hunger strike in 1980. He actively encouraged initiatives in support of the H-Block blanket men and the Armagh women. It was Fr Reid who suggested that we meet with Cardinal Ó Fiaich on the prison issue, and it was Fr Reid who persuaded the cardinal to visit the republican political prisoners on the blanket protest in July 1978.

Afterwards, the cardinal – then Archbishop Ó Fiaich – condemned the conditions under which the prisoners were being held, and said:

> Having spent the whole of Sunday in the prison, I was shocked at the inhuman conditions prevailing in H-Blocks 3, 4 and 5 where over 300 prisoners were incarcerated. One would hardly allow an animal to remain in such conditions, let alone a human being. The nearest approach to it that I have seen was the spectacle of hundreds of homeless people living in sewer pipes in the slums of Calcutta.

The cardinal informed the then British secretary of state, Humphrey Atkins, of these meetings and tried to mediate a resolution of the prison protest. It failed. The British were determined to break the prisoners.

Fr Reid was devastated by the commencement of the first hunger strike. He had lobbied ferociously for an end to the dispute. The stress of trying and failing to get a resolution of this issue took its toll and he took seriously ill. I used to visit Fr Alex in Drogheda hospital. On one occasion Colette and I found him in a very distressed state as the health of the hunger strikers deteriorated. Paradoxically, while the plight of the prisoners and their families and the ongoing conflict continued to wear him down, he took great comfort from the messages of support that the blanket men had smuggled out to him.

Some of his friends arranged to send him to Rome, where the Redemptorist main headquarters is. Fr Alec enjoyed Rome; he delighted in wandering through the city and eventually finding his way back to the Redemptorist house at nightfall. One day, on 13 May 1981, eight days after Bobby Sands died on hunger strike, Fr Alec was in St Peter's Square, reflecting on events in Ireland, the hunger strike and how different this was to Belfast, with its daily bombing attacks and intermittent gun battles. As he tried to get closer to where the Holy Father John Paul II's procession was passing an armed man dashed forward close to the *Sagart* and shot the Pope.

The *Sagart*, in a state of some understandable shock and concern for the Pope's well-being, made the mistake of recounting his experiences to friends back home. It was a story that was to be told and retold with suitable irreverence in typical black Belfast style for years after that.

It wasn't until July of the following year that the *Sagart* was allowed to return to Ireland but on condition that he didn't come north. His superiors were afraid that his fragile health could be undermined if he was allowed to become re-involved in his previous activities.

When he eventually did, we resumed our conversations about the conflict, its causes and how it might be ended. It was obvious that dialogue was the necessary first step. In the early 1980s we tried to commence a process of engagement with the Catholic hierarchy, the SDLP, and the Irish and British governments. All our advances were rebuffed. The breakthrough came after Fr Reid wrote a letter to John Hume on 19 May 1986. John phoned the monastery the next day and arrived at Clonard on 21 May.

Towards the end of 1987 we decided that John and I would begin party-to-party meetings. The *Sagart* formally wrote to both of us as 'an interested third party' inviting Sinn Féin and the SDLP to 'explore whether there could be agreement on an overall nationalist strategy for justice and peace.'

He presented us with a paper entitled 'A Concrete Proposal For an Overall Political Strategy to Establish Justice and Peace in Ireland'.

I brought the invitation to our *ard chomhairle*. It responded positively, and John and I met on Monday 11 January 1988 for several hours. For the first time our meeting was publicised and there was an immediate and generally hostile response from the governments, the other political parties and sections of the media. Jump forward twenty-five years and it is the same sections of the media and in many cases the same journalists who are still busy peddling their anti-Sinn Féin agenda.

Fr Reid never allowed any of it to distract him. He was tenacious in his pursuit of peace. He wrote copious letters to political leaders here and in Britain, and engaged in countless meetings with politicians and governments seeking to persuade them to start the process of talking. He saw good in everyone and lived the Gospel message. His was the Gospel of the streets.

He was there during the first hunger strike and became ill as a consequence of the stress. He was there during the battle of the funerals, including the funerals of the IRA volunteers killed at Gibraltar. He was in Milltown Cemetery when the mourners were attacked. Three were killed and over sixty wounded. Several days later he administered the last rites to the two British soldiers killed at the subsequent funeral of one of the victims, Caoimhín Mac Brádaigh.

Fr Reid also helped broker talks between Sinn Féin and Fianna Fáil and subsequently the Irish government and Sinn Féin. In 1999, at my request, he became involved in the ongoing efforts to locate the remains of those who had been killed and secretly buried by the IRA and others. After several years it became apparent that our initial hope that all of the remains would be located quickly was naive. He and I discussed this and consequently we put to the governments a proposal that experts in the recovery of remains, using high-tech equipment and archaeological methods, should be employed.

Later, in 2005, he was an independent witness, along with Rev. Harold Good, to the IRA putting its arms beyond use, and during this time he was also involved in trying to develop a peace process in the Basque country.

Today we brought him to his last resting place in the Redemptorist plot in Milltown Cemetery. Earlier, hundreds of his religious colleagues, political and community leaders, and the people of west Belfast attended his funeral Mass in Clonard.

The *Sagart* lived a full life. His contribution to peace in Ireland is immeasurable. There would not be a peace process at this time without his diligent doggedness and his refusal to give up. He remained through all these turbulent times a good and simple priest. He was forthright, funny and totally dedicated to upholding the dignity of human beings. He was an active proponent of equality, particularly of a woman's right to equality. He was also a proud Tipperary man and a hurling enthusiast. His last words to me were 'Up Tipp'.

Go ndéana Dia trócaire ar a anam dílis.

Do Bhí Eolas an Tslí Aige

Brendan Callanan

Prior to 1993 I scarcely knew Fr Alec Reid, but from then to 2002 I met him frequently and worked with him on the Redemptorist peace mission as much as circumstances would allow. Here I wish to mention just a few of his more outstanding qualities that caught my attention.

His innate confidence in the goodness of people was a striking characteristic of Alec. He was utterly convinced that in each and every person there was a measure of goodness that had to be appreciated and developed to enable that person make a worthwhile contribution to the community. Not everybody would have agreed with him about goodness in each and every person, but he held fast to his view and did not allow conventional protocols get in his way. A person's political or religious background made no difference to him in this regard. Some might say that he was naive and he may well have left himself open to that charge, but I hold to the contention that he was not naive but, rather, appreciative of people's goodness.

His confidence in people was, I believe, one of the factors that enabled him 'to keep on keeping on'. He had a conviction that goodness would win out, notwithstanding the disappointments experienced along the way, and there were, it may be said, many painful disappointments on the journey.

He had an extraordinary ability to communicate with people and put them at their ease, and it was always evident that when he spoke to someone he gave his complete and undivided attention. He listened carefully because he believed that in everyone there was a measure of the truth. Because he could put people at their ease, he was also able to question them and their presuppositions without causing any ill feeling. And in this he was always fair – he wanted to understand each person's point of view, get a sense of where they were coming from, but could query it because it was evident he was searching for the truth and not trying to put anyone on the spot.

Wisdom was another quality of his. There is a Gaelic expression which goes 'do bhí eolas an tslí aige'. Literally this means the person had knowledge of the way, but translates more correctly that the person learned to distinguish between what was very important and just important, between what was just important and what was not important at all, that the person had assimilated what really mattered in life. In this sense Alec was a wise person, and many of us have been the beneficiaries of that.

A profound sense of compassion was another very striking quality of his. His utter horror at witnessing any form of human suffering was easily perceived. He often used phrases like 'this cannot go on', 'what can we do about this?', 'nobody should have to go through that kind of pain'. He placed a very high value on human dignity, and any instance of that being diminished by whatever form of suffering touched him deeply. His compassion moved him to seek ways of preventing any further such suffering.

His compassion was very evident in the case of the disappeared. From 1999 onwards he was very involved in the search for nine people who had been murdered and secretly buried in unmarked graves. He was very conscious of the suffering of the families and how distressing the process was for them. Of the nine bodies, three were found almost immediately and three more in later years. His repeated visits to the families throughout the period of the searches were a testimony to his deep-felt compassion and his desire to comfort them in whatever way he could.

Alec always retained an interest in hurling, which was a passion of his from childhood. He rarely if ever missed the All-Ireland hurling final in September, and if his beloved Tipperary were playing, then so much the better. For him it was not just a sporting occasion but also a national and a cultural one. But even in Croke Park the peace mission could require time: he once met a Taoiseach under the Hogan Stand to discuss the state of play, not out on the field but a hundred miles north.

These are but a few of the qualities of Fr Alec which marked him out as a very special and unique person. It was a privilege to have known him and worked with him as a Redemptorist in the search for peace in the period 1993 to 2002.

He Had the Satisfaction of Seeing His Efforts Bear Fruit

Martin Mansergh

Many priests serving in parishes or communities torn by conflict found themselves having to mediate, trying to prevent further loss of life, ministering to the dying and the bereaved. For many years, in the 1970s and early 1980s, that was the role of Fr Alec Reid and many of his colleagues in the Clonard Monastery. As its history shows, for over a century Clonard Monastery and its priests played a very prominent role in the religious life and identity of the people of west Belfast. Its outreach has been across divides of many kinds as well as to those from within the community engaged in activities with which the Church deeply disagreed. Peace work, where trust was vital, was the most pressing social priority, and one to which a Christian perspective was directly relevant, and to which it could bring a distinctive contribution.

From the second half of the 1980s, Fr Alec began to play a pivotal role in trying to crystallise an alternative to conflict, which was characterised by a prolonged military and political stalemate with periodic and dangerous upsurges in violence. In this difficult and secret work, he had the steady support of the Redemptorist Order and the use of its facilities in Clonard, Dundalk and Dublin, in which were hosted a series of meetings between the leaderships of the SDLP and Sinn Féin, and between Sinn Féin and a representative or representatives of the Irish governing party or government leading up to the IRA ceasefire of 31 August 1994.

His role went far beyond that of a facilitator. He sought in papers of his own to analyse the situation and to put forward ideas that might act as a catalyst for movement. He met those involved individually at very regular intervals to assess attitudes, reactions and possibilities for progress. Many of the concepts he was grappling with – self-determination, human dignity and justice – were to become key components in a framework for peace. The mission he was embarked on was related to deep religious conviction about the importance of finding an alternative to conflict and about the duty of the Church to be active in seeking this.

A monastery provides a quiet and discreet setting for reflective discussion of difficult existential issues, including political ones. At the time, governments in particular were inhibited from engaging in any direct discussion with those involved with any paramilitary campaign, but a religious environment emphasised the moral purpose behind a breach of that taboo. Apart from the benefits of establishing direct communication for the purpose of exploring possibilities of peace, the challenge was to identify sufficient common ground, leaving aside the obvious and for the time being unbridgeable differences, to allow the emergence of an initiative and to enable it to progress. There were fallow periods, discouraging events on the outside, while all the time more people were being killed. While the Redemptorist Order, through its superior, kept a careful watch on what was happening, not least out of pastoral concern for Fr Reid and the strains on him, support for what he was doing was maintained, and eventually bore fruit. While other lines of communication might be interrupted, the line to Fr Reid was never down.

Fr Reid privately expressed the conviction in the late 1980s that the gun was an anachronism. It was a source of great satisfaction to him when he was chosen along with the former Methodist president Rev. Harold Good to witness the final decommissioning of IRA weapons. He had the satisfaction while he lived of seeing peace taking root. The Redemptorists can take pride and inspiration from his and their part in this achievement.

Defrosting the Paramilitaries

Ken Newell

Al Reid and I were unlikely allies in the struggle for peace in Northern Ireland. I had been a chaplain in the Orange Order and had imbibed from my loyalist background a distaste for Irish nationalism and a dislike of Catholicism. The evangelical Protestantism of my early twenties, therefore, had tilted me towards fundamentalism in belief and anti-ecumenism in terms of inter-Church relationships. It was only after a period of post-graduate theological studies in Cambridge prior to my ordination in 1968 that I began to shed much of this conditioning and recognise the reality of the Risen Christ in the Churches outside the confines of my Presbyterianism.

Alec, on the other hand, came from the deep south of Ireland and felt completely secure in his own faith tradition. When we first met in Clonard in the mid-1980s I introduced myself to him as the minister of Fitzroy Presbyterian Church in south Belfast. I was soon to discover that he was proud of his republican roots but was also keen to understand my background in unionism. In addition, one had only to mention Gaelic sports and his eyes would light up, even though it was years since he struck a hurley ball.

My earliest impressions of him were of a quiet, reserved and often inscrutable priest utterly dedicated to the needs of his people. He was small, thin, pale-faced and loved to have a smoke on a sun-drenched bench in the seclusion of the monastery garden. On those occasions when I joined him on the bench he was a charming conversationalist, and we rarely parted without his encouragement to keep on crossing the boundaries of division between the Churches and communities. Though we started out poles apart, over the next thirty years we got to know each other well, and a friendship grounded in respect and focussed on peacemaking developed.

Alec was a close friend and early mentor of his Redemptorist colleague Fr Gerry Reynolds, who joined the monastery fraternity in 1985. Gerry and I provided leadership over the next twenty-five years to the Clonard/Fitzroy Fellowship, which had been formed in 1981. Although I was less involved with Alec, he never ceased to ask us what the fellowship was up to, and on occasions he would drop in to see for himself. While I valued his support, I often noticed him sitting by himself, mulling over in his mind things he rarely ever divulged. I remained curious but did not intrude on his private musings.

Then one day I heard him speaking with a group of people about the continuing turmoil and violence in Northern Ireland. He obviously felt deeply about it. Like a dart player hitting treble twenty time after time, his clarity of mind and logic of argument seemed compelling: the only way to bring the violence to an end was by initiating a process of dialogue between all the rival groups aimed at a democratic resolution of the conflict. 'When people, including the paramilitaries, are willing to talk with each other, God is with them,' he repeatedly insisted. 'Well-intentioned state and Church condemnation achieves little or nothing. God is in the dialogue and this makes change possible.'

In 1990 Al asked me to join a small group of clergy in a private dialogue with three leading republicans from west Belfast, including the president of Sinn Féin, Gerry Adams. With the ongoing violence of the IRA showing no signs of abating, this was fraught with risks for those of us from the unionist and Protestant community.

Almost in parallel with this initiative, Alec and Gerry also persuaded me to engage with loyalist paramilitaries with whom they had already established relationships of trust. To cut a long story short, the outcome of these dialogues proved more fruitful than any of us ever dreamed of. They played a small part in the movement that eventually led to the loyalist and republican ceasefires of 1994, which paved the way for the historic Good Friday Agreement of 1997. The strength of Al's determined and often humorous friendship with the paramilitaries on both sides held us all together; the power lines of communication severed by the onset of the Troubles in 1968 were repaired, and the light of hope was once again restored.

Al was a servant of Christ who had little time for theological conversations or liturgical discourses disconnected from the harsh realities of life in Northern Ireland. He viewed them as a form of moral evasion in the face of a Gospel intended to generate a courage that ultimately enhances the health of human society.

For my part, looking back, I have no doubt that the Spirit of God was at work in Al's costly vocation to reconciliation. In many ways it tortured his spirit and ate him up emotionally. But he also lived to feel the intense joy of seeing a new day dawn, and a crucified community experience a resurrection that few believed was possible. The cross of the Most Holy Redeemer, whom

Alec served constantly, reminded him that reconciliation in a divided community is always costly and that the grace of God is free but never cheap.

Al incarnated this message on the streets of Belfast in a way that those of us who knew him will never forget. For me he was a living icon of Christian peacemaking, a friend whose faith continues to inspire, and a beloved brother in Christ whose companionship I felt privileged to share.

Sheltering the Enemy

Derek Poole

My thoughts on the life and work of Fr Alec Reid are through the lens of relational and cultural variances, but they are none the worse for that. For, paradoxically, the political and cultural differences we associate with sectarian conflict run on parallel tracks. The tragic irony for the two communities that define Northern Ireland's conflict is that we are mirror images of each other. Our estrangement and brutality is internecine precisely because we're more alike that we care to admit. We suffer from what Freud called 'the narcissism of minor difference', the spurious belief that we are incompatibly different, unable to share the common bonds of life. Even when it comes to the legacy of pain, those dreadful years of mutual killing and imprisonment, our 'narcissism' is reflected in the selective and unethical remembering of the two communities. The debate on who suffered the most and the 'hierarchy of victims' is highly politicised and contested, but in a war like ours, at some existential level, we all lost.

There was also another set of narratives and actors whose lives ran parallel with each other, and that was the work of peace-and-reconciliation activists who in the darkest years placed themselves precariously between the violent ideologies. It was in this context that I first became aware of the work of Fr Alec Reid and Fr Gerry Reynolds and their mediation and peace-building initiatives. My own work with Protestant communities in general and loyalism in particular had a strong cross-community dimension, but the 'discovery' of risky and radical Redemptorists living out their faith on the interface of sectarian hatred was an affirming mirror image that I was keen to look into.

In their Catholic peace-building initiatives I observed a number of key issues that reflected some of my own experience and also offered new and challenging insights. In particular, I was impressed by the common sense but unpractised importance of physical presence in situations of conflict and the futility of condemning violence at a safe distance. This 'theology of presence' was an essential element in the work of these men. It was a theology that not only accommodated the pastoral remit to visit prisoners and bury the dead but also to intervene in riots, forge relationships with paramilitaries, negotiate hard conversations, name the 'sins' of your own community, and, as exemplified in Fr Reid's blessing of a dead British soldier, loving your 'enemies'.

Rooted in his Irish Catholic cultural identity, Fr Reid's engagement with the IRA most certainly contributed to the end of the conflict. He had a natural affinity with his own people and understood the ideology, history and grievances of contemporary republicanism. It was this ability to be physically present, practically engaged and creatively arduous that lead to the realisation that the IRA were advocating for peace; and a Catholic priest was there to arbitrate that possibility. It would be cynical, as some have been, to dismiss Fr Reid's relationship with the IRA as 'comfortable and Catholic'. In fact, in the context of Northern Ireland, there was no love lost between the Irish Catholic Church and violent nationalism. And the image of Fr Reid forlornly stretched over two British soldiers in an attempt to 'shelter the enemy' from an IRA execution is a lived homily to where his universal loyalty lay: with humanity – made in the image of God.

A 'theology of presence' in times of conflict is easier to preach than to practise. And working with Roman Catholics like Fr Gerry Reynolds raised considerable questions for how Protestant Church leaders engaged with paramilitaries or were physically present at times of conflict. I remember conversations in Clonard Monastery and in many ecumenical forums in which it was clear that Protestant and Catholic theology created different social models for engagement and transformation. There were, unsurprisingly, strengths and weaknesses in both traditions, but the differences often lead to misunderstanding and distrust. Consequently, cross-community collaboration in vital issues like reconciliation, the nature of forgiveness and healing the past could be hindered. However, as both traditions matured through the struggle of our common hurt, two essential themes emerged that informed our peace-building practice. Firstly, that faith without justice is sterile and can make no meaningful contribution to a divided society. And, secondly, pastoral presence must be accompanied with prophetic provocation. The life and work of Fr Alec Reid helped us all understand these essentials of Christian faith.

Alec's grandfather, Alexander Reid

Three-year-old Alec

Alec's mother, Mary Reid (née Flannery)

Seminarian hurlers, Cluain Mhuire, Galway, c. 1954. Alec is at the far left, back row

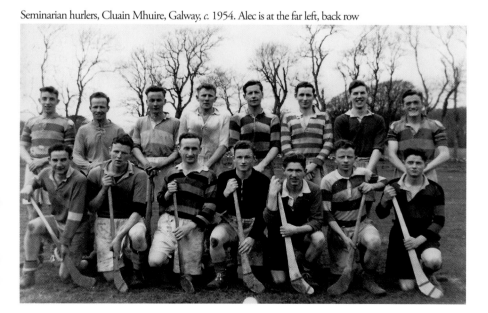

Religious profession group, 1950. Standing from left: Jim Travers, John Myers, Joe Finlay, John Lucey; seated from left: Alec, Seán McElgunn, Michael Kirwan, Peter Byrne

Fr Alec's ordination, 22 September 1957. Standing from left: Brother Harris (Alec's teacher), Alec Reid (uncle), Bridget Forde (aunt), Ita Kavanagh (aunt), George Reid (uncle), Joe Deighnan (uncle); seated from left: Mary Reid (mother), Alec, Maura Litster (sister)

Standing from left: Anne Fitzmaurice (friend), Máiréad O'Meara (niece), Margaret O'Meara (sister), Jim O'Meara (brother-in-law), James O'Meara (nephew); seated from left: Ita Kavanagh (aunt), Maura Litster (sister)

Standing from left: David Litster (nephew), Alec Litster (nephew), Donal Litster (nephew), Robert Litster (nephew), Gerard Litster (nephew); seated: Maura Litster (sister), Donny Litster (brother-in-law)

Fr Gerry Reynolds and Fr Alec at Clonard, 1980

Fr Alec with some Traveller children

© Irish News

Fr Alec with the McDonagh family at Glen Road Traveller site

Birthday greetings to Fr Alec from President Mary McAleese and Martin
McAleese

Fr Alec with Rev. Harold Good

Belfast mural dedicated to
Fr Alec

From left: Máiréad O'Meara (niece), Margaret O'Meara (sister), Donny Litster (brother-in-law), James O'Meara (nephew), Fr Alec, Maura Litster (sister), Jim O'Meara (brother-in-law), Ita Kavanagh (aunt)

A cartoon 'take' on the Nobel Peace Prize awarded to John Hume and David Trimble, with Fr Alec included

Fr Alec with Gerry Adams

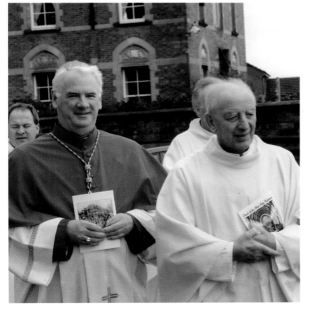

Fr Alec with Bishop Noel Treanor. This was Fr Alec's last visit to Clonard, when it reopened following its renovation in 2012

John and Pat Hume with Mark Durkan (centre)
attending Fr Alec's funeral

Sinn Féin representatives at Fr Alec's funeral

Fr Alec's funeral
at Clonard church, Belfast

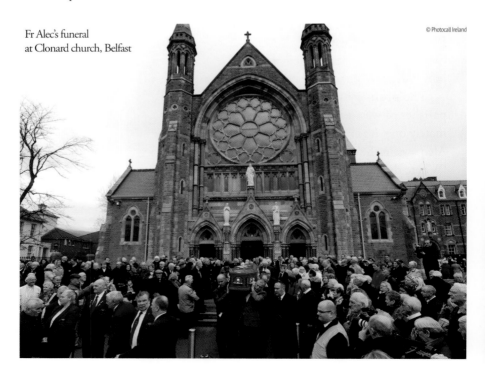

REMEMBERING A PARTNER FOR PEACE

Gerry Reynolds

I was delighted in the summer of 1983 when the Redemptorist provincial, Fr John O'Donnell, asked me to transfer from Esker, County Galway to Clonard in Belfast. I came north on 30 August with a commitment to put my energy into the work of reconciliation, letting myself be guided by the promise of Isaiah 2:2–5 that encounter with the living God is the way to peace.

Shortly afterwards, I asked Fr Alec what we could do to end the violence. 'The only way to change things,' he said, 'is through the dialogue which makes room for the Holy Spirit to work in human history.' That conversation shaped my relationship with him through the years. We shared a deep conviction that the God at work among us was master of the impossible. The dialogue must go on to prepare the way for the miracles of his grace.

Alec's work for peace is epitomised for the people by his persuasion in the early 1990s of John Hume and Gerry Adams to work together under the leadership of Albert Reynolds, Taoiseach, to create a political way forward. They have seen my role in various ways: partnerships with Rev. Ken Newell and with Rev. Sam Burch, the Protestant guest preachers on the Solemn Novena Ecumenical Day, the unity pilgrims who week by week join Protestant congregations for their Sunday worship.

The ordinary believing people who worship in Clonard and in the parishes of west Belfast connect our endeavours. For them, both are intimately one. It's all about changing some strategic relationships. Such as what Alec says in the mission statement he wrote for Cardinal Ó Fiaich in 1989: 'Where the people of Ireland in their nationalist and unionist traditions are living together in friendship and mutual co-operation for the common good of all and where the people of Ireland and the people of Britain are living together in the same way.'

It used to embarrass me that people associated me so closely with Alec. I would speak about my relationship with him as that of priest and altar server. In the narrower political sense, there is truth in that. But I know from his friends that Alec would have none of that way of speaking. I always felt a profound esteem from him. He was interested in everything we did to break down division. In the larger perspective of God's design for Belfast,

Northern Ireland and the Church among us, he saw our relationship as a creative partnership.

The response to Alec's death from such a wide range of people has increased our awareness of the significance of the Clonard Reconciliation Mission. A hundred years ago Karl Adam wrote something like this: 'The great apostolic task of the twentieth century is to cultivate a sense of the Church in the hearts of the faithful.' It remains the task of the twenty-first century. The Vatican Council says: 'The Church, in Christ, is in the nature of a sacrament – a sign and instrument, that is, of communion with God and of unity among all people' (*Lumen Gentium* 1.1). While the church at Clonard is becoming that kind of Church, we still have miles to go. Through our ecumenical endeavours we seek to make the 'sign' more compelling and politically influential. Alec would want us to become a Church that listens to, and learns the lessons from, the streets.

The reconciliation imperative covers everything we do. In this year of the Redemptorist Missionary Vocation, we need to review and renew all our relationships in order to serve more effectively God's reconciling will. We need to encourage all our brothers and sisters who celebrate the Eucharist with us in Clonard to make the unity of the Body of Christ their passionate concern.

May Alec, now that he is freer than ever he was here, help us to do just that.

PART FOUR

Documentation

Documents written by Fr Alec Reid

Letter to John Hume (19 May 1986)

Redemptorist Peace Ministry –
Mission Statement (1989)

Article in the *Irish Times*
(29 November 1990)

The Role of the Servant of Christ in a Situation
of Political Conflict (14 September 1993)

Submission to the International Body
(17 December 1995)

Letter to Senator Mitchell
(18 November 1996)

A Letter to John Hume

Clonard Monastery,
Clonard Gardens,
Belfast,
BT13 2RL
19 May 1986

Dear John,

I am writing to ask your advice with the following because it concerns what the Church may be able to do over the coming months to help the cause of peace. I am thinking in particular of what she may be able to do to persuade the IRA to end their military tactics and so to open the way to political dialogue and co-operation between all the Nationalist parties, a development which, I believe, would, in turn, open the way to new relationships between the Nationalist and Unionist communities.

I am writing personally but I know that others who are associated with me, including people of standing and influence in politics and in the Church, would agree, in principle, with the main points I shall make. To set these points in context, I would like, first, to explain that my interest is not political but pastoral and moral. I know that a priest, like the Church herself, cannot get involved in party or even nationalist politics nor can he take sides in matters of political opinion and judgment. At the same time, however, I believe that a priest, again like the Church herself, must respond to the human and moral dimensions of a political situation, especially in so far as it involves people, whoever they may be, in suffering and tragedy.

It is this tragic dimension of the situation in Northern Ireland that concerns me and that also, I know, concerns those who are associated with me both inside and outside the Redemptorist community. Whatever my private opinions may be, I am not, as a priest, either for or against any particular, political form of solution to the conflict, no matter what it might be, provided it is just and acceptable to the people as a whole.

My only aim is to help those people who, if the present situation continues, will be killed, injured or imprisoned over the next few weeks and months and whose personal tragedies will blight not only their own lives, but also the lives of those to whom they are near and dear. I can bring this explanation of my interest into sharper focus by saying that it was the death of a

U.D.R. man in South Armagh about two and a half years ago that sparked off the efforts which my colleagues and I have been making since then to end, once and for all, the violent situation which is causing such tragedies.

I have been involved in the processes of peacemaking since the Troubles began in 1969, sometimes at the level of political and Church leadership, sometimes in the prisons, sometimes across the political divide between Loyalists and Nationalists but most often at the level of the streets in Nationalist areas. Because of illness, I gave up this kind of involvement for a number of years and it was only when the UDR man I mentioned was killed and I felt that the Church and priests like myself could and should be playing a more active and effective role in ending this kind of tragedy that I became involved again. I am writing all this to explain, not only my own standpoint and interest, but also the standpoint and interest of my colleagues and associates.

Our approach is based on two principles, one of which comes from our faith and the other from our common sense. The principle of faith is that, whenever we are working for peace and reconciliation between people, we can be certain that the Lord is with us. His presence is the sure guarantee that we shall succeed if, trusting in Him and doing what we can ourselves, we keep on keeping on. The second principle, which comes from our common sense, is that the most human and the most Christian way to achieve reconciliation and peace between people who are in conflict is the way of dialogue, carried out in a spirit of respect and compassion for everyone involved. We believe that if we keep these two principles in mind and follow them out in practice, we can confidently hope to succeed.

The first principle tells us that the Lord is always with us and never more than when we are working for peace. This knowledge gives us the courage we need because it assures us that, in Him, the power to overcome every obstacle is always available to us. Keeping this principle in practice means setting our minds and our hearts sincerely on the search for peace and then going forward, sustained by our trust in His presence and His power and by the confidence which tells us that, if we do what we can ourselves, He will, step by step, light up and open the way.

The second principle tells us that respectful and compassionate dialogue is the ideal way to settle conflicts. This knowledge gives us the basic guideline that we need and points to the first steps we have to take when we set about the practicalities of making peace.

If our experiences over the past two years or so have confirmed the need for faith and the need for dialogue, they have also shown the power of these two principles when they are applied to our divisions and conflicts because, as we went along, we could see, to our great surprise, a whole scene opening up in which ways to a true and lasting peace were beginning to define themselves and which, if they had been followed up effectively as they appeared, would by now, I believe, have led us forward to a situation in which the ending of 'the armed struggle', if not actually achieved, would at least be within our grasp and where the processes of healing and reconciliation within the Nationalist community itself and, across the political divide, between the Nationalist and Unionist communities, would have been significantly advanced.

I am saying this in faith but also in the knowledge which has come from our experiences during that time when we were dealing with hard-headed and realistic people who have influence in both communities. I shall now try to summarise the results of our peacemaking efforts over the past two years and then, in view of them, outline some proposals which I would like to put to you for advice and comments.

We began by seeking the advice of people in the Nationalist and Unionist communities whose judgment we knew we could trust because of their political knowledge and experience and also because of their closeness to the actual political situation in these communities. We asked them specifically how they thought the Church could help in the search for peace.

Generally speaking, they told us that, in their view, the Church could give invaluable help because of her resources, her influence, her independence and authority and the lines of communication that were open to her. They said that, for the sake of the people of both communities, she should use these assets to define, organise and develop her pastoral responses to the causes and the effects of the conflict and that, in keeping with her pastoral role as reconciler and peacemaker in the community, she should encourage, foster and, where necessary, even initiate dialogue between the various parties and groupings who were in conflict or at odds with each other, especially when positive communication had broken down between them.

Since our main concern is to end the use of violent tactics on the Nationalist side, we spoke first to representatives of Sinn Féin, including their present leader, because we felt that they could best advise us on this issue. They told us that, in their view, the Church could play a vital role, not only in the general search for peace, but also in the creation of ways and means for ending 'the armed struggle'.

Their general opinion of the situation, at that time, was that there would be no substantial progress towards a just and lasting peace and, especially, no hope of persuading the IRA to end their campaign, unless the processes of dialogue were set up and maintained between all the parties concerned. In these, they included the Church herself because, as they saw the situation, she was in a unique position to help.

Here they referred to Pope John Paul's speech at Drogheda and said that, while everyone could recall his statement on violence, few seemed to remember what he said about the responsibilities of political and community leaders in Ireland to create peaceful but effective means for overcoming injustices so that those who were suffering from them would not be driven back on their own resources and, as a result, be tempted to justify resort to violence.

Taking their cue from this part of the Pope's speech, they said that the only way to persuade the IRA to end their campaign was to show them that the use of force was no longer necessary to achieve justice for the Nationalist community because of the availability of a peaceful strategy which, in terms of the political forces involved, could be reasonably regarded as a realistic alternative. This was the gist of the advice which the Sinn Féin representatives gave the Church representatives at the various meetings which took place between them. It was clear, therefore, to the Church representatives that, in view of this advice, the only way to achieve their aim of ending 'the armed struggle' and the tragedies that went with it, was to create a dialogue through which a powerful, political alternative could be formulated, initiated in concrete terms and then proposed to the IRA as a viable and going concern.

The representatives of the Church were naturally depressed by the implications of all this but, at the same time, heartened by the evident willingness of the Sinn Féin leadership to co-operate with them. Whatever our personal opinions might be, we realised that, to make progress, we would have to work on the possibilities which the Sinn Féin leadership had presented to us.

We, therefore, held discussions on the question of 'an alternative method' with a number of people whom we felt were in a position to advise us because of their knowledge of both the Nationalist and Unionist communities. As a result, we decided that the following proposal for 'an alternative method' should at least be explored because it was favoured by the consensus of opinion among those whom we consulted.

The essence of this proposal is that the nationalist parties, North and South, would agree, through dialogue between themselves, to formulate and, then, to co-operate in a common Nationalist policy of aims and methods for resolving the conflict and establishing a just and lasting peace. This would mean that, while retaining their own separate identities, the Nationalist parties would make an *ad hoc* agreement to combine their political forces and to act in unison in a common campaign for reconciliation and peace.

This is the theory of this particular proposal for 'an alternative method' – the creation of a powerful, combined political force on the Nationalist side to which the IRA would respond by ending 'the armed struggle' and with which they would begin to co-operate once the first serious steps to set it up were taken.

I believe that, as a theory, this proposal has a lot to recommend it. It would, for example, end the violent and tragic dimensions of the conflict which would be a blessing beyond words and which, as I have said, is the main concern of the Church. The common, Nationalist policy envisaged in this proposal would provide the Nationalist people with a powerful but peaceful base for achieving their aims; aims which would be defined and expressed in terms of a broad Nationalist consensus and which, for that reason, would be moderate, reasonable and just. This, in turn, would win respect, sympathy and support for their cause throughout the world.

Such a common, Nationalist policy would also be of great benefit to the Unionist community because, in the first place, it would end the use of arms in the Nationalist community; a tactic which must be a nightmare to them and which they so often see as sectarian in intent and motivation. It would also convince them of the need to develop new, political attitudes because, in face of a Nationalist community, so powerfully and yet so peacefully united, it would be clear beyond any doubt that real peace would never come until they came to terms, realistically and positively, with Nationalist rights and aspirations.

I also believe that such a common, Nationalist policy would be welcomed in the Unionist community by the realists among them and also by those whose political attitudes are inspired by wisdom and compassion, people who are more numerous and, at the end of the day, more influential than the 'not-an-inch' image of their community often suggests. I am not saying this off the top of my head but because of soundings I have made among Unionists and Loyalists who are sensitive to political possibilities within their own community and who responded positively and favourably to the idea of a common, Nationalist policy. This, then, is the theory of the proposal which we decided to put forward for examination and discussion.

All the time, however, it was clear that, more important than any proposal for an 'alternative method', however appealing in theory it might be, the crucial exercise in the whole enterprise would be ongoing, open-ended dialogue between all the parties concerned, that is, between the representatives of the Church as the initiators and co-ordinators of the discussions, the representatives of the constitutional Nationalist parties as the holders of the main political authority in the situation and the representatives of Sinn Féin as the party directly related to 'the armed struggle'.

The discussions we had held to date, including those with the representatives of Sinn Féin, had emphasised the primacy of open-ended dialogue as the key to the whole problem and as the *sine qua non* of progress. Without it, theories about 'alternative methods' would remain forever in the air because it would only be through the processes of dialogue, involving hard and realistic discussion and a compassionate willingness to give and take, that an alternative method to the armed struggle, acceptable to every party concerned, could be worked out and set in motion. Its form and structure, therefore, would emerge from the dialogue itself and not from any preconceived notions or theories.

At the same time, however, the representatives of the Church decided that to get the dialogue going, they should proceed on the basis of the proposal for a common, Nationalist policy outlined above because, in theory at least, this offered the best hope of progress and also because it would serve to focus the main purpose of the dialogue – the ending of the armed struggle through the creation of an alternative method.

This decision, however, did not mean that other proposals would be excluded from discussion because, from the beginning and in accordance with the principle of open-ended dialogue, the actual agenda for any meeting would be a matter for all the participants to decide. To sum up, then, on this part of the letter – our basic concern is to do all we can to remove the tragic and violent dimensions of the conflict in so far, at least, as the Nationalist community is involved.

Our reading of the possibilities of doing this at the present time is definitely positive provided that the Sinn Féin movement, in general, and the IRA in particular, can be shown that a powerful, political strategy is available as an alternative to the use of force. Indeed, my own conviction is that, if the processes of dialogue which would be necessary to create such a common policy were even initiated on a serious basis among the Nationalist parties, everyone concerned, including the representatives of the Church, the representatives of the constitutional parties and the political leadership of Sinn Féin, would be in a much stronger position than they are at present to influence the course of 'the armed struggle' and the attitudes of those who are committed to it. I also believe that, once this dialogue were underway, the IRA would begin to respond to it and to co-operate with those involved, especially the representatives of the Church.

We believe, therefore, that the resources of the Church should be mobilised to help in the creation of 'an alternative method' and we also believe that they can be mobilised provided the constitutional parties on the Nationalist side agree to co-operate. I should say here that the representatives of the Sinn Féin movement have consistently told us, over the past two years, that they will co-operate fully with the Church and her representatives in any effort they may make to promote the creation of an alternative method to the armed struggle and to substitute political methods for political ones.

They have also said that they will give the whole matter the highest priority, devote all the necessary resources and energies to it and engage, positively and constructively, in discussions and negotiations with any party or group representative, Nationalist or Unionist, and, indeed with any individual from either side, who are willing to co-operate with the Church and whose influence on the political scene places them in a position to help. They will do this at any time, without pre-conditions, either officially or unofficially, and in the strictest confidence.

As I have already said, I do not believe that it normally belongs to the pastoral role of the Church to get directly involved in the creation of political policies, although, in a situation like that under consideration here, where it is a question of creating policies which will serve as an alternative to the use of force, I believe that she should get involved in facilitating their creation. In borderline areas between political responsibility and pastoral responsibility, the nature and the degree of her involvement will depend on circumstances and judgment.

The circumstances in Northern Ireland must, I believe, be judged in the light of the fact that, since 1969, a lot of the real power to influence the course of events has been on the streets where the breakdown of normal law and order has also meant breakdowns in the lines of trust, access and communication which normally help to hold a peaceful society together. In this kind of situation, the Church has, I believe, a pastoral responsibility to intervene where she can and where others, who normally would, cannot, in order to bridge the gaps in these lines. Otherwise, the breakdowns will continue and grow worse and only soldiers and police with guns will be able to contain the situation.

This is one of the reasons why I believe the Church has a pastoral role to play in the initiation, at least, of the kind of enterprise I have been discussing and, also, in the creation of the kind of supportive and neutral setting that would be necessary to make it viable and successful.

I also believe that, in keeping with the Pope's words at Drogheda about the need to create peaceful ways for achieving justice, the Church must look again at a political situation in which, for the past sixteen years and in spite of repeated condemnations, significant numbers of her own flock have, either directly or indirectly, been involved in the determined, tragic and terrifying use of well organised military tactics to achieve political aims which have been traditionally accepted as right and just by the Nationalist community as a whole and, therefore, by the community for which the Church has pastoral responsibility.

The Church's main response to date has been to condemn these tactics as immoral but, however much this may have helped to contain the situation, it has clearly failed to end it. In addition, therefore, to moral guidance, especially when this guidance takes the form of condemnations that are not being heeded, the Church must consider what further practical responses she can make to a situation which has lasted for so long and which shows every sign of lasting into the foreseeable future.

Here, in support of the point I have been making, I would like to give some quotations from a general comment which another Redemptorist, Fr Sean O'Riordan made on a public letter which, at the beginning of last year, Mr Gerry Adams addressed to Dr Cahal Daly, the bishop of Down and Connor. Fr O'Riordan is professor of moral and pastoral theology at the Alphonsian Academy, Lateran University, Rome.

He gave me his comments on a tape and so I shall quote them verbatim.

They covered the whole letter in question but here I shall only give those that are relevant to this present letter. Fr O'Riordan said,

'I have been asked to comment on the recent open letter addressed to Dr Cahal Daly, bishop of Down and Connor by Mr Gerry Adams, Sinn Féin MP for west Belfast. I would like to begin by stating the context in which I have carefully read and studied Mr Adams's letter. The context I refer to is that of the morality or moral dimension of politics in general. From a moral standpoint what is politics? what is political activity of any kind? what is the purpose of politics and of political activity?

Politics is supposed to be the search for the good of all people in a certain geographical and human territory, smaller or larger as the case may be. Those engaged in politics are supposed to be concerned with just that – the common good, to use a very old philosophic phrase, that is, the human good of all the people who are involved in any particular form of political activity. And by involvement, I don't merely mean the activity of those who carry on politics in an active and professional manner. Those involved in politics are, above all, the people; the people, on behalf of whom or in whose name, political activity is carried on.

The essential point, then, to keep in mind in all discussions of politics is the good of people, the good of all people who are, in one way or another, involved in political activity. It was with this context and this principle in mind that I read and re-read Mr Adams's open letter to Dr Cahal Daly. My question, all the time, was – to what extent is the position stated here by Mr Adams a contribution to the common good of the Irish people and I take 'the Irish people' to include all those who live in this island and who look on this country, in one way or another, as their home.

From this point of view, I find some interesting and very positive things in Mr Adams's letter. I note, in particular, the following points:

1. In point (8) of his letter, Mr Adams addresses the following question to Dr Daly. I quote – 'you call on Republicans to renounce violence and join in the peaceful struggle for the rights of Nationalists. What peaceful struggle?' – end of quote. I think that's a very reasonable question to address to Dr Daly. And, look[ing] at things in a still broader way, I would say that people of Mr Adams's political school and, indeed, people of all political schools, have the right to address questions to those who hold responsible office in the Catholic Church.

I do believe myself that our bishops should be open to dialogue with Republicans, say, Mr Gerry Adams; with Catholics who would have other political points of view; with all Protestant political points of view, including hard-line Unionists. I do believe that Churchmen should be willing to listen to them all. This does not mean that they would take any one particular point of view put forward but, surely, it is part of the office of those who are responsible for the good of the Church, to look for the good of all people.

The Church is concerned for the good of all people, not for their spiritual good alone, in the narrow sense, but for the general good of their lives. It is in this sense, that the Church has to be involved in politics, politics being part of human life. The Church would surely be falling short of the fulfilment of its mission if it were to refuse to talk to any political school or to all political schools. That is why I do believe that Mr Adams is fully justified in addressing this letter to Bishop Daly and I think he comes up with a really good question and meaningful question in no. (8) of his letter.

2. I am also impressed by point no. (9) in the text of his letter and again I quote – 'those who express moral condemnation of the tactic of armed struggle (the armed struggle, in this case, carried on by the IRA) – those who condemn this tactic, says Mr Adams, 'have a responsibility to spell out an alternative course by which Irish independence can be secured.'

Well, I wouldn't say that it's just the business of the Church to spell out an alternative course but I do believe that the Church, officially too, should be involved in the search for an alternative course. I do believe that the Church should participate in trying to discover and formulate a course of politics, in this part of Ireland, alternative to the armed struggle, as Mr Adams calls it, being carried on by the IRA. Mr Adams adds, and I quote, 'I, for one, would be pleased to consider such an alternative.'

I am very glad that he says that. The fact that he does shows him to be not a man of fixated mind – I shall have more to say of mental fixation shortly – this shows that he is prepared to consider all strategies that could be seen as making for the common good, and, as I said at the outset, here the moral dimension of politics comes in.

From a moral point of view, the thing to be looked at in any political programme is – is this programme geared to the common good of all the people? does it make for the good of the people? In the present case, does such and such a programme make for the general good of the Irish people, of all those who live in this land and look upon it, with whatever differences of perspective, as their home.

Gerry Adams concludes this no. (9) of his letter, and again I quote, 'I know that many of my constituents, who are also lay people in your diocese, would be equally anxious to have such a strategy – (that is, an alternative strategy to armed struggle) – outlined for them.'

I would repeat that it cannot possibly be the task of the Church only to outline or to develop an alternative strategy but, certainly, the Church should take part in the search for such a strategy and I am sure that Gerry Adams is quite right in saying that, not only he, but many of those whom he represents in the constituency of west Belfast would welcome the putting forward of an alternative or alternatives to the strategy of 'armed struggle'.

Fr O'Riordan then goes on to comment, in a critical way, on some of the other points which Mr Adams makes in his letter to the bishop – I won't give them here because it would take too long and they are not really relevant to this letter. I shall, however, give a sample of them by quoting the last section of Fr O'Riordan's comments. 'I notice in point no. (6) of Gerry Adams's letter that he damns in advance or he seems to damn in advance, the present Anglo-Irish negotiations and he does so because Mrs Thatcher said that such negotiations would be based, and I quote, "on a Unionist and British agenda." Now, it's a well-known fact that, again and again, the terms that are stated at the beginning of negotiations are not those which develop when the negotiations take place. Gerry Adams addresses a question to Cahal Daly about those negotiations – 'do you believe that such negotia-tions would be in Irish interests?' Surely, the reply would be – why not try? It may be that they will come to nothing but, perhaps, something will come out of them which could serve the common good of all the Irish people.

'These, then, are my comments on Gerry Adam's letter but, again I would say that if here and there, language is used in his letter that tends to echo fanatical thinking, which I am sure is not Gerry Adams's thinking at all, but if that sort of language figures in his letter, it is in large part due to the fact that people like Gerry Adams have not been sufficiently heard and listened to. And I would say that, here again, the Church owes it, not only to Gerry Adams and to those whom he represents but to all political parties in this part of Ireland, the Church owes it to them that it will listen and will try, as far as possible, to take part in developing an alternative flexible strategy which, as far as possible, will serve the best interests of all the Irish people.'

These comments of Fr O'Riordan will help to emphasise the point I was making about the pastoral responsibility of the Church in the present political situation.

I shall now return to the account of our own efforts, especially over the past year or so, to initiate a dialogue on the creation of 'an alternative method to the armed struggle'.

After we had spoken to the representatives of Sinn Féin and they had promised to co-operate with us, it was clear that no further progress could be made without the co-operation of the constitutional Nationalist parties and, in particular, of the SDLP. We decided, however, that before approaching any of these parties in a formal way, we should seek advice on a private and confidential basis.

Some time before that, I had spoken to Mr Seamus Mallon, whom I knew personally from previous years, about the general political situation and, in particular, about the help which the Church might be able to give, at that time, to the search for peace. We decided to continue and to develop this contact through further discussion with him. As it was private and confidential, I won't go into it here except to say that Mr Mallon gave us all the advice and all the help he could in the uncertain circumstances surrounding the immediate run-up and the immediate follow-up to the Anglo-Irish agreement.

Here I should say that, apart from our contacts with Mr Mallon which, as I have said, were private and unofficial, we have never spoken, even in the most confidential way, about what we were trying to do to any other representative of the SDLP or, indeed, to any member or associate of the party who might have been able to help us.

Since last December, the matter has been out of my hands because senior colleagues were dealing with it. I wasn't free, then, to approach you or anyone else in the party during that time and that is why I didn't speak to you about it when I met you at the British and Irish conference in Oxford last January, although I would have liked, very much, to have done so. Some time ago, however, my colleagues told me I was free to take steps to continue and to develop our approach to the constitutional Nationalist parties. As the first step, therefore, I decided to write this personal and confidential letter to you to ask for your advice and guidance on the whole matter. As I have said, our crucial interest is to initiate and develop a dialogue which will aim at creating an alternative to violence, whatever that alternative might be. I shall, therefore, list some ways in which this dialogue could be initiated with a view to obtaining your advice as to which way would be the most feasible and the most likely to succeed.

1. In the first way, the Church, through her representatives, would officially invite the representatives of the SDLP and the representatives of Sinn Féin to meet, under her auspices, for discussions which would aim at creating a political alternative to the IRA campaign. The actual agenda for these discussions and the conditions under which they would take place, including conditions relating to confidentiality, would be matters for the political participants. In this first way, the primary responsibility for holding the discussions would rest with the official Church.

2. In the second way, representatives of the Church, acting with the knowledge and personal backing of her main leadership, would unofficially invite representatives of the SDLP, and representatives of Sinn Féin to meet, under their auspices, for discussions which aim at creating a political alternative to the IRA campaign. The actual agenda for these discussions and the conditions under which they would take place, including conditions relating to confidentiality, would be matters for the political participants. In this second way, the primary responsibility for holding the discussions would rest with the representatives of the Church.

3. In this third way, representatives of the Church, acting with the knowledge and personal backing of her main leadership, would unofficially invite representatives of the SDLP, to meet them for discussions on (a) the pastoral help which the Church could give, at the present time, to the search for peace, and (b) ways of initiating a political dialogue which would aim at creating a political alternative to the IRA campaign.

I should be grateful for your comments on these proposals.

I realise, however, that the best and the most efficient way to deal with a matter like this is not through letters but through personal contact and discussion and, for that reason, I would welcome an early opportunity to speak to you personally and in confidence about the points I have set out in this letter. I could go to Derry to do so, if this were more convenient for you, but I would like to see you as soon as possible because of the urgency of the matter and also because of the long delays which have already taken place. I would also like to bring one or two colleagues with me but this would not be necessary if you preferred to keep the matter on a personal and confidential basis.

If your schedule over the coming weeks doesn't allow a suitable opportunity for such a meeting, I should be grateful if you would suggest some representative or representatives of the SDLP to whom I could speak in Belfast or elsewhere, either alone or with one or two colleagues.

I am certain that, if the situation is handled properly, the IRA can be persuaded to end their campaign. I am not saying this lightly but from long experience of dealing with the Sinn Féin movement. Although I am not, and have never been, associated with them in a political sense, as they themselves would testify, I know that they trust me and understand that any contacts I have had with them were always in the context of ending violence and making peace. In this context, I have, I believe, had closer and more continual contact with them than any other priest and, perhaps, even than any other individual outside their own movement. I believe, therefore, that I can sense opportunities for making peace and I know that I can sense an opportunity now in the context of the approach I have set out in this letter.

The presence of the Church is, I believe, crucial to the success of this approach. I say this because I know that Sinn Féin and, particularly, the IRA are very wary and very suspicious of any proposals for a ceasefire and, up to now at least, would not even consider them unless they covered what they have laid down as the essential condition for a ceasefire which is, as you know, a stated intent by the British to withdraw from Ireland. The matter is very delicate, therefore, all the more because the IRA are convinced that, even if they were to call a ceasefire, there will be no lasting peace in Ireland until the British actually declare their intention to withdraw.

I believe, however, that we can cope with this situation and succeed in our enterprise, provided the Church is present all the time in a pastoral and official way. I say this for a number of reasons. The first has to do with the whole question of trust because the IRA will not enter any discussions or negotiations about a ceasefire unless they know they can trust the processes and the people involved. I am certain, however, that the witnessing presence of the Church would be a sufficient reason for them to trust and, indeed, to co-operate positively, in any discussions or negotiations about a ceasefire that would take place.

My second reason has to do with the whole position of the Church in Ireland, her moral authority and influence and, especially, the vast numbers of people who believe in her, support her and whom, therefore, she represents. The presence of the Church in negotiations about 'a political alternative to the armed struggle' would, therefore, give these negotiations a moral and pastoral stature which would be rooted in, and supported by, the attitudes of the Catholic people of Ireland as a whole. This fact alone would, I believe, have a powerful influence on the respect which the Sinn Féin movement, in general, and the IRA in particular, would have for them and, especially, on their willingness to co-operate with them.

I also believe that the Church could provide the kind of neutral and independent setting which would be necessary for the success of such negotiations.

These, then, are the reasons why I believe that the Church could play a vital and necessary role in any dialogue about 'an alternative method'.

I would like now to relate all I have been saying to the Anglo-Irish Agreement because it is, I know, the basis of present SDLP policy. The Agreement has changed the whole political situation in Ireland since we began our efforts two years ago or so but it has not, I believe, changed the need for the enterprise we are proposing or the vision or, especially, the principles on which it is based. On the contrary, it has underlined the power of these principles because, as I understand it, the Agreement is inspired by faith in the power of respectful and compassionate dialogue to heal and to reconcile even the deepest political divisions like those, for example, which exist between the Nationalist and Unionist communities.

I believe that our approach to the political divisions within the Nationalist community itself, especially those which exist between constitutionalist Nationalists and militant Republicans, should be based on the same kind of faith in the power of dialogue to heal and reconcile them.

In saying all this, I realise that the Sinn Féin party have been very critical of the Anglo-Irish Agreement and have, in fact, rejected some of its provisions. I believe, however, that their attitude to it is not totally negative and I am certain that this attitude, however negative it may be, should not be an insurmountable obstacle to any dialogue between them and the SDLP about the creation of a political alternative to the strategy of force. I say this, first of all, because, as you know, the existence of a political disagreement is one of the main reasons for having political dialogue. I also say it because I am certain that the Sinn Féin party do not see the Agreement or their political attitude to it as obstacles to a dialogue with the SDLP on the creation of 'an alternative method'. On the contrary, I believe they would see the Agreement as another reason for having the dialogue.

They have assured me, whenever I asked them, that they will enter into discussions about 'political alternatives' with the SDLP or, indeed, with any other party, without pre-conditions and on an agenda that would be drawn up by mutual agreement between the participants. I know that their leadership is shrewd and realistic enough to realise that the Anglo-Irish Agreement would be central to any discussions they might have, at the present time, with the SDLP but this has not, in any way, changed their willingness to do so. I realise that the main, indeed, the only objection which you and the SDLP have to discussions with Sinn Féin is their relationship to the IRA while the IRA are continuing their campaign. This, indeed, is another, very cogent reason why the presence of the Church would be so important to the whole dialogue because the fact that it would take place under her auspices, in the sense that she would initiate, supervise and take responsibility for it and that the SDLP, the Sinn Féin party and the other constitutional Nationalist parties would take part in it at her invitation, would, I trust, enable you and the SDLP to overcome the problem which, I know, is the problem of every constitutional politician, of the relationship between Sinn Féin and the IRA.

Finally, in relation to all I have been saying, I would like to give a personal opinion of the Unionist community. From contacts, discussions and friendships that I have had with them over the years, I believe that they are a people waiting to be redeemed from the political fears and constraints which the history of their community has imbued in them and which have crippled their best political instincts and suppressed the development of the Irish soul, which deep within their hearts and peculiar to themselves, is longing to be free. This redemption cannot properly begin or develop while, as individuals and as a community, they feel that they are under actual, physical attack from the Nationalist community. Out of respect for themselves and their own traditions, they can only, in these circumstances, close ranks and withdraw even deeper behind the emotional and political barriers they have built, through the centuries, against the Nationalist community. This situation will continue as long, at least, as the IRA campaign continues especially when so many of its targets are Ulster people. If, however, this Campaign were to end in a political reconciliation within the Nationalist community which would unite it in peaceful policies towards the Unionist community, then, at least, the way would be more open for them, not only to come out from behind their barriers, but also to grow politically into their best and native selves.

This may seem like an impossible dream, especially in the cold light of their present attitudes to the Anglo-Irish Agreement but the signs I have seen and the hints I have heard, over the years, suggest to me that, given the right circumstances, the right opportunities and the right leadership, it is not beyond the bounds of the possible. Only a time of peace will tell, and to create that time for them must be, even from the point of view of the Nationalist community, the most important reason of all for doing what we are trying to do.

This has been a very long letter but I trust you have been patient with me because of the importance of the matters it discusses, matters, really, of life and death. The deaths of the former UDR man in Newry last weekend and of Mr David Wilson at Donaghmore on Saturday, underline their importance at the present time.

I would gladly give up any further involvement in the situation because the pressures are so great but the fact that the Redemptorist community can, I believe, have an influence on it, makes me feel that, in spite of all the failures to date, we must keep on keeping on and do whatever we can to help.

I also trust that you do not think it presumptuous of me to write a letter like this to you but, as you will have seen from its contents, what we are trying to do is to define and organise our own pastoral role in the situation. Here, both you and the SDLP can be of immense help, not only in terms of advice, guidance and co-operation, but also in terms of relieving the pressures.

Our crucial need at the present time is an authoritative line of communication to the SDLP which would be constantly available to us. Belfast would clear[ly] be the best place for such a line but any arrangement which you might make for it would be very welcome and very valuable to us.

I trust, therefore, that I shall hear from you in the near future and that I shall be able to keep in contact with you, by letter at least, over the coming months.

With kindest regards and praying that God may continue to bless you with wisdom, courage and strength in the heavy responsibilities you have to carry,

Yours Sincerely,

Alex Reid C.Ss.R.

Pastoral Ministry and Political Violence

The Conflict in Northern Ireland

Redemptorist Peace Ministry – Mission Statement

Written by Fr Alec Reid in 1989
at the Request of Cardinal Tomás Ó Fiaich

The daily tragic consequences of the conflict in Northern Ireland – bloodshed, imprisonment, widespread suffering and general despair of any just and democratic solution – are a constant source of anguish to the Christian heart and demand a compassionate and effective response to it.

It is the responsibility, therefore, of every Christian but particularly of Christian leaders to do everything possible to end this inhuman situation seeking to channel the course of events away from the road of armed and violent confrontation which is strewn with death and destruction and on to the road of justice and charity and characterised by the democratic use of political and diplomatic persuasion.

We must begin by lifting our eyes to what we want to create and that, in general, can only be a new political situation where the people of Ireland in their nationalist and unionist traditions are living together in friendship and mutual co-operation for the common good of all and where the people of Ireland and the people of Britain are living together in the same way.

How to make this vision a reality is, therefore, the great question on which all our peacemaking energies and abilities must focus. For those who believe in the Christian message of justice and love, there can be only one way to do this and that is the way which begins from the fact that people are people, God's sons and daughters, before they are Irish, British, Nationalist Unionist or Republican; this means that the principles of peace are essentially the principles which respect and correspond to the human dignity and the human rights of all the people who are involved in the present conflict.

This, in turn, means that the principles by which it must be resolved are the principles of political and democratic justice as they are understood and practised throughout the world and as they pertain to the particular nature of the conflict of Northern Ireland. Rooted in the God-given dignity of the human person, these principles define 'the narrow road' which leads to political salvation. Any road defined by policies which lack the respect that is due to the dignity and the rights of people must, therefore, be seen as 'the broad road' which leads to political destruction. Here, those who believe in the Lord Jesus must be prepared, like his first followers, to leave 'all things', all their partisan and sectarian political attitudes, and follow Him down the road of democratic justice and charity to whatever political destination it may lead.

The response of the Church
Since some of the issues at stake in the present conflict pertain to the dignity of the human person and to his or her rights as a child of God and as a citizen of society, they also, by that very fact and for that very reason, pertain to the saving mission of the Church. This means that, in fulfilment of this mission, the Church must, through her representatives and ministers, intervene directly in this conflict to preach the Word of God as it applies to it and to witness to those eternal values which define, uphold and protect the dignity and the rights of the person.

It is also her mission, in face of this conflict, to preach the message of hope and courage by pointing continually to the Lord Himself as the Saviour who is always 'in the midst' with the power that can resolve every conflict and the compassion that encompasses every participant, including those who inflict injustice as well as those who are afflicted by it.

The Church, then, has a pastoral duty to respond to a political situation when (but only when) moral and humanitarian issues are at stake. Political matters, as such, which belong to the sphere of democratic opinion and choice are not her business and she has no role, from her mission, to play in them except to insist that, in all matters, the first role must be given to God-like compassion for people because it is the supreme value in human affairs and the first principle of all human relationships including those of politics.

Translated into practice, this means that the only Christian and human way to conduct political affairs and to resolve the conflicts that arise from them is the way of communication and dialogue, practised by every participant, with the respect and compassion that are due in justice and charity to every other participant.

As a process of listening and responding to what is humanly true and just in the position of every participant, political dialogue in this sense takes as its base the common humanity of all the participants and makes it the common ground where all can meet in harmony of principle to seek and to find the common good of all and, when necessary, to resolve political conflicts justly and democratically.

The Church and the dialogue of peace

Given that this kind of dialogue is the Christian and human way to conduct political affairs and to resolve political conflicts, the Church has a pastoral responsibility to use her resources, her influence and her lines of communication to encourage, promote and, when necessary, even to facilitate it.

It follows, then, that when a conflict like the one in Northern Ireland has become violent and is causing suffering and bloodshed, the Church has a missionary and pastoral duty to intervene directly and to do all she can to bring its violent dimensions and their tragic consequences to an end. Here her role may be to facilitate the necessary dialogue between the relevant parties especially when all lines of communication between them have broken down and the tragic dimensions of the conflict cannot and will not be ended unless and until they are restored. She must then use her political neutrality, her moral credibility and her own lines of communication to provide the kind of sanctuary setting where the parties to the conflict, who sincerely wish to use political and democratic methods to achieve justice and peace, can meet together for the necessary dialogue without damaging their own political or moral credibility and without compromising or appearing to compromise any of their own democratic principles.

FR ALEC REID'S ARTICLE IN THE *IRISH TIMES*, 29 NOVEMBER 1990

'Priest feels Church must provide talks channel for IRA' Reprinted with the kind permission of the *Irish Times*

As a priest who has worked in Belfast since the 1960s, my main concern is not about the political dimensions of the Northern Ireland conflict but about the tragedy it is causing in terms of human life and human suffering. It is no exaggeration to say that the people of the north have been deluged by pain and sorrow over the past 21 years and that they are still enduring a nightmare of horror, agony and tragedy.

It is natural to ask how all this could happen in a Christian country and among a people whom, in both their unionist and nationalist traditions, are I believe (and here I speak from long, personal experience) as Godfearing, as kind, as warm-hearted, as law-abiding, as hard-working, as sensitive, as gifted intellectually and emotionally as any people on this earth.

The saddest tragedy of all is that the conflict between the British unionist tradition and the Irish nationalist tradition need not and would not have erupted into violence, bloodshed and tragedy 21 years ago if the situation had been handled properly at the time.

More than this, I believe, that, even now, the violent, tragic dimensions of the conflict could be ended within any given six month period provided the situation were handled properly. I also believe that, although it has lasted for centuries, the political conflict between the Irish nationalist and the British unionist traditions could he ended within a reasonable period provided it is handled in accordance with the principles of democratic justice and charity as these principles are understood and practised throughout the world.

What are the democratic rights of the people of Ireland given that history has divided them into the people of the unionist tradition and the people of the nationalist tradition? How do you apply the principles of democracy to the present conflict especially at the point where British unionists say that Northern Ireland should be united to Britain and under British jurisdiction because this is the political wish of the majority of the people who live there, namely, the people of the unionist tradition while, at the same time, Irish nationalists say that Northern Ireland should be re-united to the rest of Ireland and under Irish jurisdiction because this is the political wish of the majority of the people who live in Ireland as a whole, namely, the people of the nationalist tradition.

These are the kind of questions which the conflict asks of everybody who wants to end it justly and democratically. Can such questions be answered? I am certain they can provided we go to the heart of what democracy means and there listen to what it tells us about the just, political and human rights of all the people of Ireland in their two divided traditions.

Why, over the past 21 years, has the conflict become so violent? The answer to this question lies in the fact that both traditions have been and still are prepared to use military force to back their own answers to the democratic questions I have just been asking. Here, however, I shall concentrate on attitudes to the use of military force within the nationalist tradition because, as a priest, my main pastoral responsibilities are towards the people of that tradition and also because it will help explain why there is so much bloodshed and tragedy.

As we know, the majority of the people of the nationalist tradition have long ago rejected the use of military force as a means of achieving their political aims, that is, as a means of ending British rule in what they see as the northern part of their country. They have decided that they will use only political and diplomatic methods to achieve this.

There is, however, within the nationalist tradition an historical heritage going back at least to the French Revolution and embodied today in the Republican movement which still believes what Irish Republicans generally used to but no longer believe, namely, that the people of Ireland have the right to use military force to resist and to end British rule and a British Government presence in any part of Ireland including Northern Ireland because, as they see it, this rule is a violation of the democratic right of the people of Ireland to rule themselves.

In spite of the opposition of majority nationalist opinion and of the continual condemnations of Church and State, the Republican movement, represented today by the Irish Republican Army and Sinn Fein, is still convinced that it is entitled to take up arms to achieve the traditional aims of Irish nationalism. At the same time, however, those who belong to this movement are also convinced that their kind of armed force could not by itself achieve these aims and, for that reason, that political methods must also be used.

What they are really talking about is pressurising the British in an efficacious way. They are saying, in effect, that they are using armed force not because they want to but because, as they see the situation, they have to; that, for them, it is simply a pressure tactic which, however unfortunate, is nevertheless necessary under present political circumstances in Ireland. If, as they say, armed force is simply a tactic to pressurise the British authorities into giving the people of Ireland their democratic rights, then you can immediately enter into a dialogue with them about replacing the pressure and efficacy of armed and violent force with the pressure and efficacy of political and diplomatic force.

A very significant fact here is that the present political leaders of the Republican movement have been publicly requesting such a dialogue for several years now and two years ago its military leaders issued a statement stating they were willing to consider proposals for 'an alternative' to 'the armed struggle' for Irish independence.

I am pointing out all this to explain why I believe the tragic and violent dimensions of what is essentially a political conflict could be ended, as far as the nationalist side of it is concerned, within any given six-month period provided it were handled properly. But it would have to be handled properly, patiently and with diplomatic skill because the people of the Republican movement who are still committed to the use of armed force belong to a military tradition that goes back for centuries and that numbers among its adherents and supporters some of the greatest heroes of Irish history.

This means that Republican convictions about the need and the justification for armed force have been handed down from generation to generation, from father to son and mother to daughter like a religious faith and so they are deeply felt and held in the hearts of Republicans.

This account of Republican convictions will, I hope, help to explain why Church condemnations of political violence in Ireland, which have been repeated again and again over the past 21 years, have not been heeded by the Republican movement and why even the passionate plea of Pope John Paul in 1979 to end the use of force for political ends was ignored.

The strange thing about all this is that, apart from their refusal to accept Church guidance on the use of arms in the cause of Irish independence, Republicans are often faithful Catholics in every other way, faithful to the Church's teachings and practices and very loyal to the Pope and to the supremacy of Rome as the See of Peter. I believe, indeed, that many

Republicans would lay down their lives for their faith as quickly as they would for their republicanism.

Why, then, do they refuse to accept the Irish bishops' and even the Pope's condemnations of their 'armed struggle'? There are a number of reasons but here I shall mention just one.

This is that the Catholic Church and the Republican movement have been encountering each other for a long time in Ireland, for centuries in fact. Republicans have learned a lot of lessons from their quarrel with the Church about the use of arms: lessons, for example, about how bishops can be affected by their own political and social backgrounds and about how the official Church can differ from the pastoral Church; lessons even about the fallibility of the Church in matters that belong, not to the sphere of faith, but to the sphere of prudential and personal judgement. Republicans have historical memories about the Church's attitudes to political questions in the past, even the distant past: memories that tend to disillusion them. The democratic principles of republicanism have taught them to think for themselves and to be independent of mind in matters of personal conscience.

Priests in Northern Ireland must, therefore, face a situation in which a significant section of the people for whom they have pastoral responsibility have taken up arms to achieve their political aims in the spirit and with the commitment and expertise of a military tradition that goes back for centuries. They have to respond to the fact that in spite of all the efforts of Church and State to persuade them to stop or to defeat them – the use of constant condemnation by the Church; the application of all the security, military and legal resources available to the London and Dublin Governments – they are continuing to use arms today.

What, in face of such a situation, should the Church do or, at least, try to do though her representatives and ministers? It is clear that, while she must give guidance on the moral issues of the conflict, pulpit-type condemnations are not enough.

Here, I believe, we can learn from the pastoral example of Jesus Himself. He is always 'the Lord who is with us', the Saviour who is 'in the midst', the Friend who is 'like unto us in all things except sin.' He communicated directly with those whom He wished to influence including people who were condemned by the official Church of the time as the worst of sinners and outlaws. He sat down to table with them and engaged them in personal dialogue so often and so much that He became known by what I believe is His greatest title: 'The Companion of Sinners' – of the sinners that we all are.

The pastoral approach of Jesus indicates, I believe, that the Church must enter into direct communication and dialogue with the Republican movement if she wants to persuade it to abandon the gun and to follow the ways of peaceful politics. My own experience has taught me that, if the Church does this, she will find that the Republican movement is open, not only to such communication and dialogue, but also to such persuasion.

I believe, for example, that, given the necessary communication with the other political parties or authorities that would be concerned, the Republican movement could be persuaded to end its strategy of armed force in favour of a strategy of political force or even of new, realistic ways of defining and applying the democratic principles that should govern the just resolution of the present conflict.

I am convinced, however, that the Republican movement will not be persuaded to give up its armed strategy for a political strategy unless it has first been satisfied that such a strategy would be organised enough and strong enough to pursue effectively the broad thrust of the traditional aims of Irish nationalism in the political setting of the 1990s. Such an efficacious political strategy could, I believe, be set up but only if the main political parties on the nationalist side of the conflict and the main Republican movement agree to pursue it together because only then would it have the kind of political force behind it that would satisfy the Republican movement.

At the present time, however, there is no communication between the main nationalist parties and the Republican movement because these parties refuse to communicate with it while it is engaged in an armed campaign. This means that a political strategy acceptable to the Republican movement as a replacement for its armed strategy cannot be organised at present and will not be unless and until the necessary lines of communication between it and the other nationalist parties are set up. Here the Church could play a crucial role because, for pastoral and moral reasons, she could, and, I believe, should intervene to facilitate the creation and the organisation of these lines of communication and, by doing so, help to promote a dialogue which, at the end of the day, would, I am convinced, remove the gun forever from the nationalist side of the age-old conflict in Ireland.

I can sum up all this by saying that there is a tragic impasse at the heart of the peace-making process in Northern Ireland. It has been created, on the one hand, by the insistence of the Republican movement that it cannot and will not lay down its arms in favour of any new proposals for justice, reconciliation and peace unless and until it has been able to verify the political viability of such proposals through unconditional communication with the other political parties and authorities who would be involved in implementing them. On the other hand, it has been caused by the insistence of these parties and authorities that they cannot and will not engage in any kind of political communication with the Republican movement unless and until it lays down its arms.

How to resolve this impasse is, therefore, one of the crucial questions for peace in Northern Ireland. My own conviction is that it cannot and will not be resolved unless and until the Church, in keeping with her pastoral responsibilities in any situation of violent conflict, intervenes through her representatives and ministers, to provide the kind of sanctuary setting where the lines of communication necessary to resolve it can be set up and maintained.

THE ROLE OF THE SERVANT OF CHRIST IN A SITUATION OF CONFLICT

Lecture Given by Fr Alec Reid, Clonard Monastery, Belfast, 14 September 1993

As I see it, the role of the servant of Christ in a situation of conflict is to be the pastoral agent of the Holy Spirit in the midst of the conflict. I say 'in the midst of the conflict' because there and there only can he come to grips with all its human and, consequently, all its moral and spiritual dimensions, and it is the moral and spiritual dimensions of the conflict that are the business of the serving Christian.

I can spell this out by saying that a conflict exists when people on a personal or community basis disagree, oppose, confront or even attack each other. Their motives for doing so are always human and, because they are human, these motives and the conflicts to which they give rise always have moral dimensions of goodness and badness.

This means that there are moral questions at the heart of every human conflict and the crucial role of the Christian is to identify those questions and then to answer them in accordance with the Spirit of Christ. In other words, he must, under the guidance of the Holy Spirit, answer them as Christ would answer them, no matter what the personal or community consequences may be.

To achieve this, the serving Christian must stand in the middle of the conflict and encounter it in all its flesh-and-blood reality until he comes to understand it with the knowledge of direct, personal, front-line experience because this is the only kind of knowledge which will enable him, with the help of the Holy Spirit, to identify the moral dimensions of good and evil which are involved in causing and driving the conflict. In other words, he must know the conflict 'from within' rather than 'from without' because only then will he be able, with the Spirit's guidance, to grasp and to come to grips with all the moral issues which must be resolved if the conflict itself is to be resolved in a Christian way.

This brings us to the truth which defines the meaning and guarantees the effectiveness of the role of the serving Christian in a situation of conflict, the truth, namely, that, at all times and in every situation, he is the pastoral agent of the Holy Spirit. This is a truth too awesome almost to contemplate and certainly beyond our human understanding, but it is the truth, never-theless, which, by enveloping him in the power of the Holy Spirit, creates the spiritual environment which alone can sustain and enable him as he strives to fulfil his mission at the pit face of the conflict situation.

That mission, as I have already indicated, is to discern all the moral issues to which the conflict gives rise and then to take up a clear-cut, leadership position on each of them which in a just, reasoned, but, at the same time, compassionate way, conforms to the moral values of the Lord Jesus and which, therefore, enables him to point the way to a Christian resolution of the conflict.

It is a daunting mission, to say the least, especially when you relate it to the conflict in Northern Ireland with all the moral issues it presents to us in the context of its long history of division, confrontation and violence.

It is clear, therefore, that the serving Christian could not face such a mission in Northern Ireland or, much less, accomplish it without the Holy Spirit and the power which He alone can give us. The glorious truth, however, is that, thanks to the mission which Jesus Christ accomplished in the conflict situation of His own life on earth, all of us, both as individu-als and as communities, have been endowed with the Holy Spirit and the gifts which come from communion with Him; gifts, for example, like the understanding, the wisdom, the prudence, the courage, the spirit of patient endurance and, especially, the spirit of compassionate love which are crucial to the role of the serving Christian in a situation of conflict.

I am stressing the relationship between the role of the Holy Spirit and the role of the serving Christian in conflict resolution because I believe that the Christian will not survive, let alone succeed, at the pit face of the conflict, especially in Northern Ireland, unless he is inspired by the conviction that the Holy Spirit is always with him and is sustained by the confidence in His enabling power which flows from that conviction. This assures him that, whatever opposition he may have to face, whatever the problems, setbacks, deadlocks, mistakes, disappointments and failures, the Holy Spirit will always be able to counter them, always able to change disadvantage into advantage, threat into opportunity, the negative into the positive just as He changed the Cross of Jesus into the victory of the Resurrection. Fortified, then, by his faith in the abiding and dynamic presence of the Holy Spirit, the serving Christian in a conflict situation learns, as he must, to live by the confident conviction that, however great or even impossible the adversity he has to face may appear to be, there is always a way through, always a way out, always a way forward which he will find if he waits on the Spirit's guidance and relies on His saving power. A relationship of personal trust in the Holy Spirit, developed through constant communication with Him and constant reliance on Him, is, therefore, central to the role of the serving Christian in a situation of conflict.

I would like now to illustrate what I have said so far from the example of Jesus. How did He accomplish His role as the agent of God in the conflict situation that is human life?

By living in the midst of it until He became bone of its bone and flesh of its flesh. In other words, He identified personally and continuously with the conflict situation which is the story of His life; allowed Himself to get completely caught up in all its dimensions of good and evil, from the level of the individual to the level of those who wielded political and religious power, but always as the agent of God's justice and, especially, of His compassion. As a result, He became embroiled and, in the end, fell victim to the violence, both moral and physical, which is endemic to so many situations of human conflict.

For me, all this is summed up by St John in one sentence: 'The Word was made flesh and lived amongst us' (Jn 1:14). This, I believe, is the crucial scriptural guideline for the serving Christian in a situation of conflict. He must, like Jesus, become personally involved in its full humanity until he knows it by heart in all its flesh-and-blood reality.

I would like to develop this point by saying that Jesus came to create companionship between God and humankind on a personal and community basis and among humankind on the same basis; a companionship which, through the gift of the Holy Spirit, would be as close as the Divine Companionship which exists within the Trinity of God. It is not surprising to find, therefore, how much Jesus used companionship as a means of exercising His pastoral influence and leadership. I would like to stress this aspect of His pastoral ministry because I believe it has special, indeed, crucial significance for the role of the Christian in a situation of conflict.

I am using the word 'companionship' instead of similar words like 'friendship' or 'fellowship' because, in its original meaning, it relates to a favourite, indeed, classical strategy of the pastoral ministry of Jesus.

I say this because, as we know, the word 'companion' derives from two Latin words which mean 'one who eats bread with another'. The word 'companionship' connotes, therefore, the kind of sharing which takes place between people when they gather around a common table to eat and drink together; a sharing, consequently, which, of its very nature, involves not only the food and drink which nourish the body but also the personal conversation and dialogue which nourish the spirit of understanding, reconciliation, intimacy and friendship between the participants; in a word, the kind of relationships which inspire personal and community companionship.

Given its natural dynamic for developing these relationships, Jesus often used the table of food and fellowship around which this dynamic comes into force. The fact that he saw it as an ideal setting for explaining and, indeed, symbolising His message and for exercising His influence and leadership proves and, at the same time, illustrates that the creation of companionship was a central strategy of His saving mission.

The fact that a pastoral genius like Jesus used the strategy of companionship so much in His ministry is, I believe, full of significance for the role of the Christian in a situation of conflict, especially when we take into account the all-inclusive nature of the companionship He practised.

The story of His mission shows that Jesus was prepared to share His company with anybody who was prepared to share his or her company with Him, no matter how good, bad or indifferent their relationships with God and their fellow men and women might be. This is clear from what people said about Him. For example (if I may paraphrase a little), 'This man welcomes tax-collectors, that is, people who oppress us and who are the enemies of His own people.' 'This man eats and drinks with all kinds of disreputable people, including prostitutes.' 'This man is the companion of all kinds of sinners.'

Jesus practised human companionship to the point of being called 'a glutton and a drunkard' and of getting Himself a bad name for keeping bad company. He practised it in a way which shocked many people, including, at times, His own disciples; in a way, indeed, which, if we really think about it, tends to shock even ourselves.

To those who accused and even rejected Him for associating with the wrong kind of people, Jesus, as we know, gave various replies, including for example the parable of the Pharisee and the publican, with all its implications for not being judgmental about anybody whose personal conscience before God we do not and, indeed, cannot fully know.

We remember His classical response to those who brought the woman accused, under Jewish law, of the capital offence of adultery – 'Let the person who is without sin be the first to move against her' – a challenge, as we know, which caused all her accusers to disappear.

We remember also the parable about the two debtors which He told to Simon the Pharisee because he was shocked when Jesus allowed a woman of bad reputation to wash His feet with her tears and dry them with her hair: 'I have something to say to you, Simon.' And the 'something' he had to say was the point of all His replies to those who accused him of associating with sinful company: 'Which of you is without sin?'

Taking our cue, then, from the example of Jesus, we may say that the crucial role of the Christian in a situation of conflict must be to create companionship with all the participants through ongoing communication and dialogue with them. The Christian, therefore, cannot say: 'There are some people in this conflict with whom I will not associate because I regard them as sinful participants', since to do so would clearly contradict the example of Jesus. Equally, however (and for me this is a crucial point), the Christian cannot say: 'I shall limit my role in this conflict to those whom I regard as the sinful participants', because this would mean ignoring the message of Jesus, quoted above, that sinfulness is universal, with all the implications that message has for the moral attitudes and positions of every participant in a situation of conflict.

In other words, if the Christian in a situation of conflict does not engage or, at least, seek to engage in communication, dialogue and companionship with all the participants, he will not understand and so will not be able to address all the moral issues which will have to be resolved before the conflict itself can be resolved in a Christian way.

I would like now to apply what I have said so far to our own conflict in Northern Ireland. Following the example of Jesus, the central strategy must be to create compassionate companionship with all the participants who are in the midst of the conflict by engaging in direct, ongoing communication and dialogue with them. The aim of this would be to identify the moral and spiritual dimensions of their various positions with a view to deciding on a Christian pastoral response to each of them.

The extent to which the Christian ministry can accomplish that will be the extent to which it will succeed in fulfilling its mission at the pit face of the conflict situation. That mission, as I have already indicated, is to discern all the moral issues to which the conflict gives rise and then to take up a clear-cut, leadership position on each of them which in a just, reasoned, but, at the same time, compassionate way conforms to the moral values of the Lord Jesus and which, therefore, enables the ministry to point the way to a Christian resolution of the conflict.

I would like now to spell out what I see as the practicalities of achieving all this.

- The first step would be to list all the participants in the conflict and to grade them according to their significance for its resolution.
- The second step would be to meet authoritative representatives of all the participants with a view to explaining the role of the Christian ministry to the conflict and to persuading them to cooperate with it.
- The third step would be to set up a programme for pursuing the strategy of the ministry in an organised, dynamic and, therefore, effective way.

There are some other practical points about this ministry which I would also like to mention. The first is that it is essentially a ministry of communication – the kind of communication which is characterised by the spirit of compassionate Christian dialogue. It would be impossible here to discuss the full dimensions of this dialogue and so I just wish to stress that it is the very life of the Christian ministry of conflict reconciliation, and that its first and crucial activity is to listen – to listen in a spirit of Christian compassion and discernment to the viewpoint of the party or group with which the ministry is in dialogue.

The purpose of this listening is to understand the political position being explained with a view to discerning the elements of moral truth and justice contained in it. These elements qualify for the pastoral affirmation and support of the Christian ministry. Those involved in the ministry seek to identify the area of moral truth and justice which is shared in common by all the participants and which, therefore, constitutes the common ground where the resolution of the conflict can be achieved.

Listening is consequently crucial to the process of resolving a political conflict because it is by listening to the conflict itself that one discovers the formula for peace. In other words, the way to peace is to be found within the conflict itself and, as experience has shown, can only be found there. Experience has also shown that it can always be found there provided those who are seeking it listen to the conflict in the way described above, that is, in a spirit of Christian compassion and discernment.

This approach is based, as I have said, on experience but also on what I have already called the crucial scriptural guideline for the serving Christian in a situation of conflict, namely: 'The Word was made flesh and lived amongst us.' The implications of this for our own situation is that: 'The Word has become flesh in the conflict in Northern Ireland and lives in the midst of it.' I say this because this is the Jesus in whom we believe, our Emmanuel – 'The God-who-is-with-us' – the Lord who, yesterday, today and forever, is the same. We may say, therefore, that the role of the Christian in a situation of conflict is to meet Jesus in the midst of it and to listen to Him there.

Translated into practice, this means that whenever and wherever within the conflict, the serving Christian, with the help of the Holy Spirit, hears the word of truth, the word of justice, the word of compassion, he is hearing the words of Jesus and listening in effect to the message of Jesus for the resolution of the conflict. This is another way of saying that where truth is, where justice is, where compassion is, Jesus is, a truth of our faith which is reflected and confirmed by the statement of 'Where love is, God is.'

I believe, therefore, that in the light of this truth and in response to it, the Christian ministry should take the following kind of step-by-step approach to its dialogue with all the participants of the conflict.

- Identify the elements of moral truth and justice in the party position which has been explained and then set them out in writing with reasons for accepting them as such.
- Identify any elements in the position explained which would not be compatible with the principles of moral truth and justice and then set them out in writing with the reasons for not accepting them.
- Give the representatives of the party concerned a written response to their explanation of their party's position with a view to developing the dialogue with them. This response would set out: the points of agreement and the points of disagreement between the Christian pastoral position and the party position. The dialogue would then concentrate on the points of disagreement with a view to sorting them out and reaching more and more agreement between the two positions.
- Inform each and all of the parties to the conflict of the elements of moral truth and justice which the Christian reconciliation ministry had discerned and which it would support in the political positions of the

other parties, and then ask for an authoritative response to this information from each party.

By proceeding in this way, the Christian ministry would promote the whole dialogue of peace by creating understanding across the political divisions which are causing the conflict and help to uncover and identify the common moral ground between all the parties to the conflict – the only ground where agreement and reconciliation can be established.

Give leadership to the ordinary faithful by keeping them informed in an ongoing way of the progress to date of the dialogue of peace between the Christian reconciliation ministry and all the parties to the conflict. The purpose of this information would be to gain the spiritual and moral support of the people to promote the dialogue of peace among them and to preach the message of Christian hope in a conflict where they are often tempted to despair.

When you think of the role of the servant of Christ in a situation of conflict, you are forced, I believe, to think of a special ministry of Christian reconciliation and companionship which needs the endowment of special charisms by the Holy Spirit. This reminds us of the understanding of the Christian Church expressed by St Paul when he said that Christians are called by God to various kinds of ministries and empowered to fulfil them by the Holy Spirit through special gifts which grace them for the responsibilities of each ministry and which are bestowed on both a personal and community basis.

When you reflect on the role of the servant of Christ in a situation of conflict like the one in Northern Ireland, you are forced, I believe, to think in terms of a special ministry of Christian reconciliation carried out by a team of men and women, clergy and laity, who have the time, the skills, the experience and, especially, the stamina for such a demanding mission, a team which, ideally, would be representative of all the Christian traditions in Ireland.

Submissions From Fr Alec Reid C.Ss.R
to the International Body
(Chaired by Senator George Mitchell)

17 December 1995
Clonard Monastery,
Belfast BT13 2RL

Dear Senator Mitchell,

I was a witness to all the negotiations and agreements between the Irish Government, the SDLP and Sinn Féin that led to the IRA cessation of the 31st of August, 1994 and the inauguration on the 6th of September, 1994 of the new alternative strategy by the Taoiseach, Mr Albert Reynolds TD, the Leader of the SDLP, Mr John Hume MP MEP and the President of Sinn Féin Mr Gerry Adams.

In circumstances where I would have to act as such a witness I shall always testify in an honest, independent and forthright way. To do otherwise would be to dishonour the integrity of the Quid Pro Quo Accord and the sanctity of the nationalist commitment to the principles of democratic and peaceful politics which that Accord represents and embodies. It would also dishonour the integrity of the pastoral ministry for peace which I have been conducting for many years with the support of the Redemptorist Community at Clonard Monastery, Belfast, and the approval of the Redemptorist Provincial Superior, Very Rev. Brendan Callahan C.Ss.R. and his predecessor, Very Rev. Raphael Gallagher C.Ss.R.

I hereby submit four documents to the International Body.

Document No. 1
Submission on the Decommissioning Issue in the Context of the Quid Pro Quo Accord between the Irish Government, the SDLP and Sinn Féin. (16 pages)

Document No. 2
The IRA Cessation and the 'Alternative Democratic Consensus' Strategy as defined by the Terms of the Quid Pro Quo Accord between the Irish Government, the SDLP and Sinn Féin. (4 pages)

Document No. 3
The Significance of the Meeting between the Taoiseach, the Leader of the SDLP and the President of Sinn Féin at Government Buildings, Dublin, on the 6th of September, 1994. (16 pages)

Document No. 4
The Test Issue of the Peace Process. (5 pages)

I trust that this submission will be of help to the International Body as it carries out its arduous and demanding task.
Yours Sincerely,
Fr Alec Reid C.Ss.R.

Submission on the Decommissioning Issue in the Context of the Quid Pro Quo Accord Between the Irish Government, the SDLP and Sinn Féin

Personal Note

In providing this commentary, I write as a participant in and a witness to all the discussions and all the communications, verbal and written, between the Irish Government and Sinn Féin, and also between the SDLP and Sinn Féin, which led eventually to the IRA cessation of 31st August 1994 and the meeting between the then Taoiseach, Mr Albert Reynolds TD, the leader of the SDLP, Mr John Hume MP and the President of Sinn Féin, Mr Gerry Adams at Government Buildings, Dublin on the 6th of September 1994.

Fr Alec Reid C.Ss.R.

Clonard Monastery,

Clonard Gardens,

Belfast BT13 2RL

The IRA cessation is based on a Quid Pro Quo Accord between the Irish Government, the SDLP and Sinn Féin. The terms of this Accord and the commitments they embody are set out in Document No. 1. There is a relationship of complete interdependence between the stability of the IRA cessation and the faithful fulfilment of all the essential terms of the Accord.

Consequently, all the commitments embodied in those terms are relevant to the work of the International Body. Some of them, however, have a particular relevance because of their relationship to the issue of 'decommissioning' or 'demilitarisation' and for that reason, I would like to draw special attention to them. They include the commitments set out under Sections 1, 2, 3, 6, 7 and 11 of the Accord.

Sections 1, 2 and 3 of the Accord state:

1. The overall objective of the new strategy would be the democratic resolution of the conflict achieved through dialogue, negotiation and

agreement between all the political parties with the necessary democratic mandate and the British and Irish Governments.

2. Round-table dialogue and negotiations between all the democratically mandated parties and the British and Irish Governments would provide the essential format through which the new strategy would move forward towards its objectives.

3. The resolution of the conflict would take the form of a new political settlement which would respect and therefore accommodate the democratic rights of the people of both the Unionist and Nationalist traditions and create a healing environment for all the divided relationships which have been historically at the heart of the conflict.

The peacemaking principles set out above under Sections 1, 2 and 3 of the Accord define the core of the 'Democratic Consensus' between the Irish Government, the SDLP and Sinn Féin on which the Nationalist 'alternative' strategy for peace is based. (For the significance of the word 'alternative', as used here, see Document 3.) It will be seen, then, that the principles which define the methods, format and overall objective of this new Nationalist strategy are essentially principles of human and, consequently, of democratic justice. This means that they are rooted in and spring from the God-given dignity of the human person with all the rights and freedoms, both individual and communal, which flow from and are defined by that dignity. It follows, therefore, that the spirit of the Nationalist strategy is completely democratic: that its special genius, so to speak, is to be able to encompass the whole spectrum of political tradition in Ireland in a way that respects, affirms and accommodates the democratic values and the unique identity of every strand of it.

The spirit, then, which inspires the Nationalist strategy and which gives it the outreach that can embrace the values and concerns of every political tradition in Ireland, which is truly democratic, is the spirit which looks first of all to the human dignity of the people who form each tradition and the rights that belong to that dignity with a view to ensuring that those rights will be upheld, protected and affirmed during the whole process of dialogue, negotiation and agreement through which the conflict will be finally settled.

If we translate the sense of this into what it means for the people of the Unionist community in Northern Ireland, we shall see that the Nationalist consensus strategy is designed to protect and to affirm their human and democratic dignity and the political and cultural identity which is uniquely their own, as much as it is designed to protect and affirm the human and democratic dignity and the political and cultural identity of the people of the Nationalist community.

It belongs to the very essence of the Nationalist 'Democratic Consensus' strategy that, in an all-inclusive way, it should be able to embrace, confirm and accommodate the democratic rights and freedoms of the people of both communities and the variety of political and cultural gifts which grace the traditional identity and the historical heritage of each of them.

It follows, therefore, that, in the spirit of justice which characterises its whole approach to the resolution of the Nationalist–Unionist conflict, the Nationalist consensus strategy has the democratic capacity to merge with any peace consensus which the Unionist community may decide to make their own, provided it also were inspired by the same spirit of justice.

This does not mean, however, that, in the event of a merger between a democratic Unionist consensus and a democratic Nationalist consensus for peace, there would be a consequent blurring or fudging of the identities which belong to Unionists and Nationalists as two distinct communities with historical, political and cultural traditions of their own.

On the contrary, the achievement of a democratic Nationalist–Unionist consensus for peace would free the people of both communities from fear and hostility which have bedevilled their historical relationship and release them into a new world where the true spirit of each community would flourish in that friendship where the affirmation of the other's unique identity becomes the finest expression of one's own.

The fact that the consensus which defines the Nationalist strategy for peace was consciously and deliberately designed to deliver a democratic objective by means of a democratic agenda (as is clear from the description of it given above) should be carefully noted because it is crucial to a proper understanding of that strategy.

The fact that it emerged from the Nationalist side of the conflict may incline people to think that its aim, per se, is to achieve a settlement of the conflict which would be in keeping with the traditionalist objectives of historical Nationalism. It is clear, however, from the principles that define the framework and the dynamic of the strategy that such a depiction of it would be a false one; false to its spirit and to the imperatives of democratic justice which must govern its methods and its objectives.

For the same reasons, it would be false to allege that it is a pan-Nationalist front or conspiracy designed to create a juggernaut of political forces which would coerce the people of the Unionist community in Northern Ireland into a sectarian styled political society where they would be dominated by Nationalist ideology and subject to 'Nationalist imperialism'.

The fact is that the exact opposite is true because, as the 'democratic consensus' which defines it clearly demonstrates, the Nationalist strategy is not in any way designed to violate the democratic dignity or to coerce the rights and freedoms of the people of any community, whether it be Unionist or Nationalist, British or Irish.

To sum up then: the Quid Pro Quo Accord was developed by the SDLP, Sinn Féin and the Irish Government in order to remove the gun forever from Nationalist politics by means of a new strategy which would serve as a 'democratic alternative' to the historical tactic of the 'armed struggle' because it would represent and, therefore, be energised by their consensus on the democratic principles and procedures which must govern the resolution of the conflict.

Dialogue, practised in all its dimensions as the truest and most enriching form of human communication, constitutes the essential *democratic method* of the Nationalist 'alternative' strategy because it is the essential democratic method of peaceful politics and the crucial *sine qua non* dynamic of conflict resolution.

A lasting peace settlement achieved through round-table dialogue and negotiation between all the parties to the conflict, based on their agreement and in keeping with the justice which is due by democratic right to the people of the Unionist and Nationalist communities and the people of Ireland and Britain, constitutes the *democratic objective* of the Nationalist 'alternative' strategy.

The common or consensus support of the people of the Nationalist community in Northern Ireland, combined with the support of the Irish Government and the assistance of the international community, particularly in countries like the USA where there is an influential Irish diaspora, constitutes the *democratic dynamism* which, under the consensus leadership of the Irish Government, the SDLP and Sinn Féin, empowers the ongoing effective implementation of the Nationalist strategy for peace.

It is clear, then, that the peaceful activities which constitute the fundamental agenda of democratic politics everywhere, namely, dialogue, negotiation and agreement, also constitute the fundamental agenda of the Nationalist peace strategy.

The *implementation* of this Nationalist agenda by the Irish Government, the SDLP and Sinn Féin, working together on the basis of a consensus approach which focuses the enabling support of the people, North and South, whom they represent, constitutes the peaceful, democratic 'alternative' to 'armed struggle'.

Section 6 of the Accord states:

6. Sinn Féin would be treated exactly like any other political party in Ireland and any mandate given to them by the people would be fully recognised and respected. They would not be subject to any pre-condition over and above the pre-condition already fulfilled by the IRA cessation for their full participation in the round-table dialogue and negotiations between all the democratically mandated parties and the British and Irish Governments through which the conflict would be settled.

The commitment embodied in Section 6 of the Accord is the ultimate *sine qua non* foundation of the IRA cessation. Any attempt, therefore, either direct or indirect, by any of the parties to the Accord to change or water down that commitment would constitute a breach of the Accord which could only undermine that foundation. If any of those parties were to persist in such a policy, the Accord would inevitably collapse and with it the foundation of the IRA cessation. The commitment of Section 6 of the Accord is guaranteed by the word of honour of the parties to it. It follows, therefore, that if any of those parties were to seek, either directly or indirectly, to force a change in Section 6, they would be in breach of that honour and consequently of their own integrity.

Section 7 of the Accord states:

7. In the pursuit of a democratic resolution of the conflict, no political party would have a veto over the holding of peace talks, the progress of peace negotiations or any democratically agreed outcome of those negotiations, whatever form the outcome might take.

The commitment embodied in Section 7 of the Accord is fundamental to the integrity and, consequently, to the stability of the Accord itself.

Consequently, if any of the parties to the Accord were to renege on this commitment, or to attempt, either directly or indirectly, to force a change in it, they would breach the Accord in a way that would inevitably lead to its collapse.

The commitment of Section 7 is guaranteed by the word of honour of all the parties to the Accord. It follows, therefore, that if any of these parties were 'to renege on that commitment or to seek, either directly or indirectly, to force a change in it, they would be in breach of that honour and, consequently, of their own integrity'.

Section 11 of the Accord states:

11. All issues relating to the militarised dimensions of the conflict would be resolved in the context of the agreement by which the conflict itself would be resolved through a new political settlement.

The commitment embodied in Section 11 of the Accord is fundamental to the integrity and consequently to the stability of the Accord. The issue of 'decommissioning' or 'demilitarisation' (as it was then called) was discussed and decided by the Irish Government, Sinn Féin and the IRA before the IRA cessation through the system of communication then in place. As a full participant in that process of discussion and as a witness to the decisions taken, I would like to make the following statement about it. To understand all the connotations of the agreement on 'decommissioning' or 'demilitarisation' which is set out under Section 11 of the Accord, it is necessary to place it in the context of the dialogue that led to the Quid Pro Quo Accord and the IRA cessation.

This dialogue began in 1987 when the Leader of the SDLP, Mr John Hume MP MEP agreed to meet the President of Sinn Féin, Mr Gerry Adams, to discuss a new agenda for peace.

The background to their meeting was the failure for so long (generations, even centuries) to settle the Irish conflict by means of peaceful politics. The violent eruption of that conflict in Northern Ireland from 1969 onwards focused this failure to a point where it became imperative to respond to it. That is what the two Northern leaders and with them the Irish Government (who participated indirectly in their dialogue from the beginning) set out to do from 1987 onwards and that is why the Accord they agreed between themselves in 1994 is so fundamental to the future of peace in Ireland.

From the beginning, the overall objective of the SDLP and Sinn Féin leaderships (representing the Nationalist community in Northern Ireland) and the leadership of the Irish Government (representing the people of the Republic) was to remove the gun forever from Nationalist politics by creating a new, democratic and peaceful strategy based on and consequently energised by the consensus support of the people whom they represented, North and South.

This new strategy could then be presented to the IRA and the military tradition they represent in Irish history as 'an alternative' which, given the age-old conviction on which that tactic is based, they could accept as credible and realistic. The Sinn Féin leader told his SDLP counterpart and also the Irish Government that unless such a replacement strategy were provided, it would be impossible to persuade the IRA to end their campaign.

From start to finish, therefore, over all the years during which it continued, the dialogue between the leaderships of the SDLP, Sinn Féin and the Irish Government turned on the question of how to take the gun out of Irish politics forever. This was the question which motivated and focused their whole dialogue for almost a decade; it was the overriding objective which inspired the agenda of every contact, every communication and every meeting that ever took place between them.

Given the presence of the gun in Irish politics for so many centuries and the long historical failure to settle the Irish conflict by means of peaceful politics, the task of removing the gun completely from the political landscape of Ireland was a formidable one, so formidable indeed that it seemed to be virtually impossible.

It looked, so to speak, like a chasm too wide to bridge, especially when that chasm represented the kind of fundamental division which for generations had separated the 'physical force' tradition from the 'constitutional' tradition in Irish history.

The presence, however, of Mr Adams in the dialogue, his conviction that the task could be accomplished and his personal commitment to doing so encouraged the other participants to persevere on the way to their objective which he had pointed out to them, the way, namely, of the 'alternative' principle. In practice, this meant that the IRA could be persuaded to end their campaign in a way that would remove the gun forever from Irish politics if they were presented with a new strategy based on democratic principles which would apply the dynamics of peaceful politics to the conflict in a way that would be powerful enough to ensure steady progress towards a just but lasting settlement; in other words, a strategy which would have the inbuilt political and peaceful capacity to change the situation from one of division and conflict to one of peace, reconciliation and justice for all the parties concerned.

The enterprise was, however, so fraught with political risk, personal danger, communication difficulties and the need to heal the deep-seated enmity and mistrust which for so long had characterised relationships between the 'physical force' and 'constitutional' traditions, that it took many years of hard-slog processing before the three leaderships were able to agree on a set of principles which would provide both the framework and dynamic for a peaceful and democratic strategy that, in the view of the Sinn Féin leadership, could be presented to the IRA as a credible and realistic 'alternative' to 'armed struggle'.

The dynamic which would focus and drive the democratic strategy and the principle from which this would spring were the crucial elements of the agreement. It was clear that any proposal for an 'alternative' strategy however democratic or detailed in form, and however much Mr Hume and Mr Adams might agree on it would lack all reality and, consequently, would not be worth the paper it was written on if it did not contain a dynamic with the capacity to drive it forward towards its objective. It would have no credibility therefore with the IRA and, consequently, no chance of winning the acceptance as an 'alternative' to the 'armed struggle'.

The reason for this was the significance which the IRA attached to the dynamic of their 'armed struggle' in the context of the historical Anglo-Irish conflict. For them, the fundamental cause of this conflict, and of all the tragedies that flowed from it, was the historical refusal of the British Government to recognise the right of the Irish people to democratic self-determination. It followed, therefore, in the IRA's view, that the recognition of this right by the British Government was the only basis for a just and lasting settlement of the conflict. This meant that for the IRA the primary responsibility for peace in Ireland lay with the British Government.

This analysis went hand in hand with the conviction rooted in the historical tradition to which they belonged that the British Government would not concede on the issue of Irish self-determination unless they were pressurised into doing so. From the IRA's point of view, therefore, it was imperative to challenge the British Government on their responsibilities to peace in

Ireland by means of a dynamic which would at least make them face up to those responsibilities.

The IRA's position turned, therefore, on the need for such a dynamic if the conflict were to be resolved or, at least, if movement towards its resolution were to be steadily maintained. How to provide this dynamic was consequently the key question for the IRA. Influenced by the historical attitudes and experiences of the military tradition to which they belonged and persuaded by the failure, as they saw it, of peaceful politics to protect the human and democratic dignity of the Nationalist community in the North during fifty years of Unionist domination under British Government control, the IRA was convinced not only about the need for an effective dynamic if the conflict were to be resolved but also that such a dynamic could only be supplied by a strategy which had a military dimension to it. In other words, they were convinced that any realistic strategy for a democratic peace in Ireland would have to be driven, in part at least, by a military dynamic. This conviction was the reason behind their 'armed struggle' and that was why they regarded it as a necessary tactic in the search for peace in Ireland.

Whatever may be one's opinion of this analysis, the fact is that it was there and that it explained both the existence of the IRA and the military campaign which they were then conducting. The two leaders had no choice but to engage this IRA position if they were to make any headway towards persuading them to end their campaign.

They did so by distinguishing between the decision to opt for 'armed struggle' and the conviction which motivated it: the conviction, namely, that any real strategy for resolving the Anglo-Irish conflict must contain an efficacious dynamic, that is, a dynamic with the inherent capacity to hold its own against all the forces, whatever they might be and wherever they might come from, which would try to block the progress of the strategy and prevent it from reaching its objective.

It was clear, therefore, that any proposal for a purely peaceful and political 'alternative' to 'armed struggle' would have to come to terms with this IRA conviction in the sense that it would have to embody a principle which, as far as possible, would guarantee a dynamic with the capacity to maintain the focus and the momentum of the strategy.

From beginning to end, therefore, the dialogue between the leader of the SDLP and the President of Sinn Féin turned on the question of how to create a purely political strategy for peace in Ireland which would have the credibility to convince the IRA that it contained the dynamism for progress towards success, however gradual that progress might be.

What the two leaders had to do, then, was to meet the challenge to the efficacy of peaceful methods of conflict resolution in the Irish situation which was presented to them by the IRA's armed struggle and the centuries-old conviction about the need for military methods which lay behind that struggle.

They set out, therefore, to define the principles of a purely political strategy for peace which, in their view, as the responsible leaders of the Nationalist community in Northern Ireland, would enshrine a dynamic with the necessary effectiveness for success.

The leadership of the Irish Government co-operated with the leaderships of the SDLP and Sinn Féin from the beginning of their dialogue and, given the political circumstances of the time, actively contributed as much as it could by bringing the expertise and the dynamism of its own political will and commitment, as the Sovereign Government of the people of the Republic, to bear on the development of the common democratic enterprise for peace which had been initiated by Mr Hume and Mr Adams.

After several years of contact, communication and dialogue between the three leaderships, they reached a consensus based agreement on a set of principles which would provide both the framework and the dynamic for a purely political and democratic strategy for peace.

This strategy was presented to the IRA leadership as a credible and realistic 'alternative' to the tactic of 'armed struggle'. They accepted it as such and, as a result, agreed to call the complete and definitive ending to their military campaign which was announced on the 31st of August, 1994.

To understand the full explanatory context of the agreement in Section 11, it is necessary also to relate it to the Irish Government's *sine qua non* stipulation for the Quid Pro Quo Accord.

This, in substance, was that the Irish Government would not enter into any peacemaking Accord with Sinn Féin unless, as a prior and absolute condition, the IRA had decided to end their military campaign. It would have to be a complete and definitive ending (to quote the description used by the Irish Government) because otherwise the Irish Government could not and would not agree to any form of understanding with Sinn Féin. An open-ended ceasefire, for example, or any kind which would be tied to a duration

of time however long, was never countenanced by the Irish Government
nor was it ever mentioned by Sinn Féin throughout all the communication
on the peacemaking Accord which took place between them prior to the
31st of August, 1994.

There was no fudge, therefore, or equivocation about the Irish
Government's insistence on the absolute need for a total cessation of the
IRA's campaign before they would make any form of peace agreement with
Sinn Féin. As they saw it, the cessation would have to constitute a watershed
in Irish history in the sense that it would mark the beginning of a new era in
Irish conflict resolution: an era, that is, which would be characterised on the
Nationalist side by a 'democratic consensus' approach to the settlement of
the conflict and the consequent removal of the gun forever from Nationalist
politics. This insistence on the principle of durability was fundamental,
therefore, to the Irish Government's position in all the communication with
Sinn Féin which culminated in the IRA cessation. It was also one of the
main reasons why this communication took so long to achieve that result.

Sinn Féin, therefore, were left in no doubt whatsoever about the
definitive nature of the cessation to which the IRA would have to commit
themselves and which would have to be in place before the Irish Government
would make any commitments to Sinn Féin or agree to any Quid Pro Quo
peacemaking Accord with them.

The Sinn Féin leadership gave long and careful consideration to the
Irish Government's position on this issue, so much so that at one stage they
became concerned about the ability of a present-day IRA leadership to make
commitments which with certainty would control what future generations
of Republicans might or might not do. This concern was resolved for Sinn
Féin when the Irish Government told them that the IRA leadership would
not be bound to what was humanly impossible.

To make sure that the wording of the cessation announcement would
conform exactly to the position of the Irish Government, Sinn Féin asked
the Irish Government to give them in writing the kind of wording which
they wanted the IRA to use. The Irish Government agreed and then forwarded written and verbal advice to Sinn Féin which identified the key
terminology that, from their point of view, should define the IRA cessation.
The IRA leadership accepted this advice without demur and incorporated
the proposed terminology in the draft of the IRA cessation statement. They
then sent a copy to the Irish Government for their comment and approval.

The Irish Government gave their approval but suggested the addition of another key word because, in their view, it would help to clarify the nature of the IRA cessation. The IRA leadership accepted this suggestion. Then to ensure that it accorded with the wishes of the Irish Government, the IRA leadership sent them the final draft of the announcement with a covering verbal message.

This message went through the announcement sentence by sentence and explained the reasons for the statements contained in them. It showed how the IRA leadership had followed the advice of the Irish Government on the terminology which defined the IRA cessation. It confirmed that the IRA leadership wanted the announcement to say what the Irish Government wanted it to say.

This covering message also stated that the commitments made by the IRA leadership in the cessation announcement were guaranteed by the word of honour of the IRA and that the fulfilment of those commitments would prove the integrity of that word and that bond of honour. The Irish Government approved the final draft of the cessation statement and the IRA leadership were informed that they had done so.

It will be seen, then, that the crucial terminology which defines the IRA cessation in the statement of the 31st of August, 1994 was not only approved but in fact provided by the Irish Government.

In summary, then, the *sine qua non* for the Irish Government of any Quid Pro Quo Accord, agreement or commitment between themselves and Sinn Féin was the complete and definitive ending of the IRA's military campaign.

What the Irish Government sought, therefore, was a decision by the IRA to end their campaign once and for all and then a public pledge to that effect based on their word of honour. Once that had been done, the Irish Government for their part would implement the political arrangements for the development of the peace process which, in accordance with the understanding between themselves, the SDLP and Sinn Féin, they had already promised as a Quid Pro Quo for the IRA cessation.

For the Irish Government, then, the sufficient but crucial guarantee of the IRA's commitment to end their campaign was their word of honour, truly given. The Irish Government's decision to accept this guarantee as sufficient was based on their confidence that the leaderships of both Sinn Féin and the IRA would be faithful to their word of honour. This confidence was in turn based on the historical evidence for such faithfulness and also on the Irish Government's own experience of several years of indirect dealings with the Republican Movement.

The IRA leadership did exactly what the Irish Government had requested them to do as the starting term for any Quid Pro Quo peacemaking Accord between themselves, the SDLP and Sinn Féin when they announced the cessation on the 31st of August, 1994.

It will be seen, then, that the agreement of Section 11 and the other decisions relating to 'decommissioning' or 'demilitarisation' set out below were made in the context of a Nationalist peace initiative designed to remove the gun forever from Nationalist politics on the basis of a new 'alternative' strategy for a democratic resolution of the conflict which is now defined by the terms of the Quid Pro Quo Accord. It will also be seen that the agreement and the decisions in question relate to a context where the complete and definitive cessation described above would have been put into place by the IRA.

As a result of the process of communication on the specific issue of 'decommissioning' or 'demilitarisation' which took place between the Irish Government, Sinn Féin and the IRA, prior to the IRA cessation, the following arrangements were decided and agreed.

1. The IRA would not be asked to hand up or to destroy weapons as a condition for the implementation of the Quid Pro Quo Accord provided they had committed themselves to a complete and definitive ending of their military campaign and given a public pledge to that effect.

2. IRA weapons would have to be kept under the strictest control in order to ensure that they did not fall into the wrong hands and become a source of gangsterism. Through Sinn Féin, the IRA gave an explicit assurance to that effect to the Irish Government.

3. The Irish Government's policy on IRA weaponry would not be affected by the IRA cessation. Their security forces would, therefore, continue as before to search and, as far as possible, to capture them. The IRA understood the Irish Government's position on this and expressed no reservations about it.

4. In the negotiations that led up to the IRA cessation, the Irish Government suggested to the IRA through Sinn Féin that, at some stage after the cessation was in place, they should demonstrate their good

faith in a symbolic way by destroying some weapons. In their response through Sinn Féin, the IRA leadership said that the suggestion was not feasible. The Irish Government understood and accepted this position in a direct, unambiguous and very definite response which I personally heard and to which, therefore, I was immediate witness.

The political and, in particular, the psychological dimensions of persuading the IRA to end their campaign must also be taken into account because they too had a bearing on the way the Irish Government handled the 'decommissioning' issue before the cessation of August, 1994. Here, the first fact to note is that it took seven years of intense dialogue between the Irish Government, the SDLP and Sinn Féin before the IRA could be persuaded to call that cessation. In doing so, they were going against all the instincts and convictions of the Republican tradition to which they belonged; instincts and convictions which, however much their violent expression may have been condemned, were nevertheless strong and deep-rooted enough to motivate the greatest personal and family sacrifices.

In 1994, the IRA, as an organisation, had just come through 25 years of such sacrifices and through the trauma which those sacrifices and the experiences of an horrific conflict had imposed on them. True, this trauma was directly related to the campaign they had conducted during that time but, in assessing that fact, it must be kept in mind that, from their political point of view, this campaign was justified because its objective for them was to secure the free and independent exercise of the democratic right of the Irish nation to self-determination.

In taking this approach, they were motivated by the conviction which had been the historical *raison d'être* for the militarist Republican tradition to which they belonged. This conviction maintained that the British Government, for reasons of self-interest, would never allow the free and independent exercise of that right to self-determination unless they were forced by a military dynamic to do so.

There was also the fact that, in 1994, the IRA had not been and, according to expert military opinion at the time, could not, be defeated. This meant that, as an organisation, they had to be persuaded to end their campaign. The difficulties of doing so were compounded by the failure of the 'Feakle' ceasefire of 1974. As an organisation, the IRA regarded this ceasefire as a debacle, not only because it failed to produce fruitful peace negotiations but also because they were convinced that the British Government had made tactical use of it for 'counter-revolutionary' purposes. As a result, they became unyielding in the determination that they would never again call a ceasefire of any duration unless and until the British Government had declared its intention to withdraw from Ireland. While they were always prepared to talk about peacemaking to any party that was prepared to talk to them, they would not call a ceasefire under any circumstances outside the context of a British 'declaration of intent'. Those who tried to persuade them to do so from 1975 onwards will know how adamant and intransigent they were on this issue.

When the Pope, for example, in the late eighties, asked warring groups everywhere to mark a World Peace occasion by calling a one day ceasefire, the IRA refused to respond. They also refused the ceasefire requests made repeatedly over the years by the British Government, the Irish Government, the SDLP and the Churches.

It is also relevant to keep in mind that the British and Irish Governments, in spite of using all the security, political and economic resources available to them, could not over 25 years defeat the IRA. The Churches condemned their campaign on an almost daily basis to no avail. We may recall, for example, how the Pope, on his visit to Ireland in 1979 'went down on his knees' (as he put it himself) 'to beg' the IRA to stop their campaign, but even this appeal was ignored. The almost countless peace groups and movements which were formed in Northern Ireland from 1969 onwards made no impact on the IRA's determination to continue their campaign until the British Government announced their intention to withdraw.

I could go on to show how many initiatives taken in secret over the years to persuade the IRA to call a ceasefire (sometimes just for Christmas) failed because of their closed attitude to any such suggestion. (It is notable, for example, that, during the seven years of the dialogue between Mr Hume, Mr Adams and the Irish Government, the IRA did not call even a token ceasefire until the three-day ceasefire of Easter, 1994.)

I think, however, that I have given a clear enough picture of the political and psychological background to the decisions made by the Irish Government on the issue of decommissioning before the IRA cessation, and also to the related agreement set out under section 11 of the Quid Pro Quo Accord.

The policy on decommissioning embodied in the agreement of section

11 was a *sine qua non* condition of the IRA cessation. It was, therefore, fundamental to the IRA's decision to call that cessation. For that reason, it is also fundamental to the integrity, and, consequently, to the stability of the Quid Pro Quo Accord.

Any attempt therefore by any of the parties to the Accord to force a change or to water down the agreement of section 11 would constitute a breach of the Accord that could only undermine its stability. If any of those parties were to persist in such a policy, the Accord and with it the basis of the IRA cessation would inevitably collapse.

The commitment embodied in section 11 of the Accord is guaranteed by the word of honour of each of the parties to it. It follows, therefore, that if any of those parties were to seek to force a change or to water down the commitment, they would be in breach of their own honour, and, consequently, of their own integrity.

The IRA Cessation and the 'Alternative, Democratic Consensus' Strategy as Defined by The Terms of the Quid Pro Quo Understanding Between the Irish Government, the SDLP and Sinn Féin

Personal Note
In providing this commentary, I write as a participant in and a witness to all the discussions and all the communications, verbal and written, between the Irish Government and Sinn Féin, and also between the SDLP and Sinn Féin, which led eventually to the IRA cessation of 31st August 1994 and the meeting between the then Taoiseach, Mr Albert Reynolds TD, the leader of the SDLP, Mr John Hume MP and the President of Sinn Féin, Mr Gerry Adams at Government Buildings, Dublin on the 6th of September 1994.
Fr Alec Reid C.Ss.R.
Clonard Monastery,
Clonard Gardens,
Belfast BT13 2RL

The IRA Cessation and the Quid Pro Quo Understanding
The definitive decision by the IRA to call a complete cessation of military operations is based on a Quid Pro Quo Understanding between the leaderships of the Irish Government, the SDLP and Sinn Féin. The objective of this Understanding is to remove the gun forever from Nationalist politics in Ireland. Consequently, there is a relationship of complete interdependence between the stability of the IRA cessation and the faithful fulfilment of all the essential terms of that Understanding. It is crucial, therefore, to have a clear understanding of what those terms mean in practice.

The first and fundamental term for the Irish Government was that the IRA would have to call a complete and definitive ending of their military campaign before the Irish Government would agree to implement this Quid Pro Quo Understanding between themselves, the SDLP and Sinn Féin.

The vital terminology which defines the IRA cessation in their announcement of the 31st of August, 1994 (including the words 'definitive' and 'complete') was provided by the Irish Government at the request of Sinn Féin and used by the IRA in that announcement.

The IRA leadership fulfilled exactly what the Irish Government had requested of them as the first and fundamental condition for the implementation of the Quid Pro Quo Understanding between themselves, the SDLP and Sinn Féin when they announced their cessation of the 31st of August, 1994.

With the IRA cessation in place, the way was open for the immediate implementation of the new democratic 'alternative' strategy for settling the conflict which had already been agreed between the Irish Government, the SDLP and Sinn Féin as the quid pro quo for that cessation.

The Democratic 'Alternative' Strategy

The terms of the Quid Pro Quo Understanding between the Irish Government, the SDLP and Sinn Féin which defined the new democratic 'alternative' strategy were as follows.

1. The overall objective of the new strategy would be the democratic resolution of the conflict achieved through dialogue, negotiation and agreement between all the political parties with the necessary democratic mandate and the British and Irish Governments.
2. Round-table dialogue and negotiations between all the democratically mandated parties and the British and Irish Governments would provide the essential format through which the new strategy would move forward towards its objectives.
3. The resolution of the conflict would take the form of a new political settlement which would respect and therefore accommodate the democratic rights of the people of both the Unionist and Nationalist traditions and create a healing environment for all the divided relationships which have been historically at the heart of the conflict.
4. The Irish Government would set up a Forum for Peace and Reconciliation as soon as possible.
5. All political parties with the necessary democratic mandate including, therefore, Sinn Féin, would be eligible to participate in the round-table peace negotiations.
6. Sinn Féin would be treated exactly like any other political party in Ireland and any mandate given to them by the people would be fully

recognised and respected. They would not be subject to any pre-condition over and above the pre-condition already fulfilled by the IRA cessation for their full participation in the round-table dialogue and negotiations between all the democratically mandated parties and the British and Irish Governments through which the conflict would be settled.

7.   In the pursuit of a democratic resolution of the conflict, no political party would have a veto over the holding of peace talks, the progress of peace negotiations or any democratically agreed outcome of those negotiations, whatever form that outcome might take.

8.   Once the IRA cessation was clearly in place, the policy of the Irish Government would be that they and the British Government would use the authority vested in them under the terms of the Anglo-Irish Agreement to set a date and to issue invitations for round-table peace negotiations between all the democratically mandated parties and themselves.

9.   If (as feared by Sinn Féin) both Unionists parties refused the invitation to the round-table all-party peace talks, the two governments would have no choice but to fall back for the time being on a vigorous implementation of the Anglo-Irish Agreement through the Inter-Governmental Conference as the format through which they would move the peace process forward towards a democratic settlement of the conflict.

10. The Irish Government would implement a positive and generous policy on the release and repatriation of prisoners and the repeal of the emergency legislation and would seek to persuade the British Government to adopt the same policy on these and other issues like the dismantling of security fortifications and the re-opening of cross-border roads.

11. All issues relating to the militarised dimensions of the conflict would be resolved in the context of the agreement by which the conflict itself would be resolved through a new political settlement.

12. Pending a new settlement, the SDLP, Sinn Féin and the Irish Government would co-operate on all issues relating to the protection of the human and democratic dignity of the Nationalist community in Northern Ireland so as to ensure equality of treatment and parity of esteem.

13. The *implementation* of the new strategy outlined above by the Irish Government, the SDLP and Sinn Féin working together *on the basis*

of a consensus approach to achieve its objectives, particularly its overall objective of a democratic settlement reached through inclusive dialogue and negotiation would constitute the essential 'alternative' to 'armed struggle'.

This *consensus* approach by the Irish Government, the SDLP and Sinn Féin to its implementation would provide the dynamic which would drive the new strategy forward towards its democratic objectives. The commitment by the Irish Government, the SDLP and Sinn Féin to implement the new 'alternative' strategy outlined above by means of the new 'alternative' dynamic described above was symbolically signed into place by the public meeting between the Taoiseach, Mr Albert Reynolds TD, the Leader of the SDLP, Mr John Hume MP MEP and the President of Sinn Féin, Mr Gerry Adams which took place at Government Buildings, Dublin, on the 6th of September, 1994.

The Significance of the Meeting Between The Taoiseach, the Leader of the SDLP and the President of Sinn Féin at Government Buildings, Dublin on 6 September 1994

Personal Note
In providing this commentary, I write as a participant in and a witness to all the discussions and all the communications, verbal and written, between the Irish Government and Sinn Féin, and also between the SDLP and Sinn Féin, which led eventually to the IRA cessation of 31st August 1994 and the meeting between the then Taoiseach, Mr Albert Reynolds TD, the leader of the SDLP, Mr John Hume MP and the President of Sinn Féin, Mr Gerry Adams at Government Buildings, Dublin on the 6th of September 1994.
Fr Alec Reid C.Ss.R.
Clonard Monastery,
Clonard Gardens,
Belfast BT13 2RL

The Significance of the Meeting between the Taoiseach, the Leader of the SDLP and the President of Sinn Féin at Government Buildings, Dublin on the 6th of September, 1994
The political and historical significance of the meeting which took place between the then Taoiseach, Mr Albert Reynolds TD, the leader of the SDLP, Mr John Hume MP MEP and the President of Sinn Féin, Mr Gerry Adams at Government Buildings, Dublin on the 6th of September, 1994 should be carefully noted because it is fundamental to a proper appreciation of the Quid Pro Quo Understanding on which the IRA cessation is based. An account of the facts which surrounded the meeting will help to explain this significance.

It was directly related to the IRA cessation which began five days before on the 1st of September, 1994 because the agreement to hold it with all the symbolism it carried was a *sine qua non* condition of that cessation. This fact alone indicates the cardinal significance which the leaderships of the Irish Government, the SDLP, Sinn Féin and the IRA attached to it.

Generally speaking, then, the meeting symbolised the official response of the Irish Government, the SDLP and Sinn Féin to the IRA cessation.

Seen in that light, it marked a crossroads in the history of Irish nationalism where a new accord between two of its oldest and most bitterly divided traditions was symbolically signed and sealed. There was, on the one hand, the 'physical force' and, on the other, the 'constitutional' tradition – to give them the historical names which broadly describe the crucial distinction between them. Both of them are centuries old. Some indeed would say that the tradition of 'physical force' is as old as the first armed battle ever fought in Ireland between the native and the foreigner.

Be that as it may, the tradition has been a part of Irish history for a very long time and its *raison d'être* has always been directly related to the Anglo-Irish conflict and the methods needed to settle it in a just and lasting way. According to its analysis of this conflict, the issue at stake was the democratic dignity of the Irish nation. England's historical policy towards Ireland constituted an ongoing violation of this dignity because it was a policy of conquest designed to protect and promote the interests of English imperialism. The Irish nation, therefore, had an inalienable right in justice to resist this policy by political means but also, if its people so decided in accordance with that right, by the use of physical force. In support of this analysis, its proponents argued that English policy in Ireland was imposed and sustained by the use or, at least, the threat of physical force.

It followed, therefore, that the resolution of the conflict would have to embrace this division between Nationalists and Unionists in a way which would respect the democratic dignity and accommodate the political and cultural identities of the people of both traditions.

It was clear that such an accommodation could not be imposed by any form of coercion which would violate the dignity or seek to undermine the identity of either the Nationalist or the Unionist community. This meant that, for the proponents of the 'constitutional' tradition, the tactic of physical force was completely ruled out by the democratic demands and the on-the-ground realities of resolving the conflict.

The process of discussion, dialogue and negotiation which led to the IRA cessation of the 1st of September, 1994 and the meeting five days later between Mr Reynolds, Mr Hume and Mr Adams embodied, at its core, the age-old debate between the 'constitutional' and the 'physical force' traditions of Nationalist politics in Ireland.

The nature of the conflict, the democratic issues at stake in it and the capacity of peaceful politics to resolve it in a way that would be just to all the participants were the crunch issues of the agenda.

In the debate, the position of the 'physical force' side was represented by the IRA's attitude to the conflict while the position of the 'constitutional' side was represented by the attitude of the SDLP and the Irish Government. Sinn Féin facilitated the debate by acting as the main intermediary between the two sides, a role for which they were particularly suited and which they fulfilled very successfully because of their association with and understanding of the political philosophy which has been the historical source of the rationale and the motivation of the 'physical force' tradition.

In the end, the outcome of the debate turned on the issue which had always been at the heart of it – how do you endow a Nationalist strategy for a democratic peace with the necessary efficacy to succeed? Or, to put it in another way – how do you create a Nationalist strategy for peace with a dynamic powerful enough to drive it forward towards a democratic resolution of the conflict?

This was the question which in the past had marked the point where the two traditions had divided in confrontation and divorce. Now, however, thanks to the reaching out which had inspired the dialogue between Mr Hume and Mr Adams, it became the point where they found the common ground on which they could meet in harmony to build a new relationship of trust, agreement and reconciliation.

This common ground was uncovered when the representatives of the two traditions agreed in principle that any realistic strategy for the democratic resolution of the Irish conflict must contain the kind of political dynamic or driving force which would enable it to maintain a steady onward course towards that objective in spite of all the adversity and all the hostile counterforces which the enterprise of peacemaking in Ireland must inevitably encounter.

This concurrence on the need to empower the new peacemaking strategy which was the objective of their dialogue with a political dynamic of the calibre that would ensure its democratic efficiency in face of all the *Realpolitik* challenges of conflict resolution in Ireland was the catalyst for the unique historical rapprochement between the 'physical force' and the 'constitutional' traditions which opened the way to the Quid Pro Quo Understanding on which the IRA cessation is based.

This Understanding turned on the *quid pro quo* equation of removing one dynamic on condition that it would be replaced by another in an honourable and equitable exchange. There was, on the one hand, a military, and on the other, a peaceful dynamic. The military dynamic was embodied in the campaign which the IRA had been conducting for twenty-five years and also in their determination to continue it until the British Government acknowledged that the Irish nation had the democratic right to self-determination.

The peaceful dynamic which, in accordance with the Quid Pro Quo Understanding, was to replace this military dynamic would be constituted by and embodied in the common-will or consensus support which the people of Nationalist Ireland, North and South, acting in unison under the direction of their elected leaderships, would give to the new, democratic strategy for peace which had been formulated as a result of the dialogue between the SDLP, Sinn Féin and the Irish Government.

Generally speaking, then, the understanding was that the IRA would remove the military dynamic represented by their campaign from the Nationalist side of the conflict by ending that campaign on a permanent basis on condition that it would be replaced immediately by the peaceful dynamic described above which, under the consensus management of the Irish Government, the SDLP and Sinn Féin, would serve as a democratic, quid pro quo 'alternative'.

In accordance, therefore, with that condition, this 'alternative' dynamic would provide the driving force for the new, peacemaking strategy which had been formulated by the SDLP, Sinn Féin and the Irish Government on the basis of an agreement which embodied the consensus of their three leaderships.

This consensus defined the democratic principles which would govern the methods, the format, the dynamic and the overall objective of the new strategy. These constituents of the strategy are set out as follows in the Quid Pro Quo Understanding.

The Methods of the 'Democratic Consensus' Strategy

The 'democratic consensus' defines the methods of the new, 'alternative' strategy as the methods of peaceful and democratic politics.

This means that, by agreeing to support this strategy, the leaderships of the Irish Government, the SDLP and Sinn Féin have formally committed themselves to pursue its peace objectives, at all times and under all circumstances, through the exercise and only through the exercise of the skills and tactics of political dialogue and diplomatic persuasion which constitute the very essence and the dynamic driving force of peaceful and democratic politics.

It follows, therefore, that the 'alternative' strategy will be empowered to move forward towards its objectives with the necessary focus, drive and momentum through the use and only through the use of the dynamics which come into play when the skills of politics and diplomacy are expertly practised.

This commitment to the methods of peaceful politics also means that, in the implementation of the 'alternative' strategy, none of the participating parties will use or countenance the use of any tactic which would violate or seek to violate the freedom of consent which belongs by democratic right to the people of the Unionist tradition and the people of the Nationalist tradition in Ireland.

The Format of the 'Democratic Consensus' Strategy

Round-table dialogue and negotiations between all the democratically mandated parties and the British and Irish Governments will provide the essential format through which the new 'alternative' strategy will move forward towards its objectives.

The 'Alternative' Dynamic of the 'Democratic Consensus' Strategy

The basis of political power in a democratic society is the common or consensus will of the people who form that society. Their own common or consensus will-power is, therefore, the generative source of the political dynamism through which alone they can move forward in a peaceful and democratic way towards the achievement of their common goals as a society.

This definition of the dynamism of peaceful and democratic politics is given here because it is also the definition of the 'alternative dynamic' on which the IRA cessation is based. As a democratic principle, therefore, it describes *the nature* of the 'alternative dynamic' which, in accordance with the Quid Pro Quo Understanding between the Irish Government, the SDLP and Sinn Féin, would replace the 'military dynamic' of the 'physical force' tradition if the IRA were to end their campaign.

This consensus between the three leaderships on the definition of the 'alternative dynamic' was developed during the dialogue which set up their

Quid Pro Quo Understanding. It corresponded to the *historical argument* which the 'constitutional' side in that dialogue used to counter the *historical argument* which the proponents of the 'physical force' side had traditionally put forward to prove the need for a military dynamic on the Nationalist side of the conflict: the argument, namely, that the methods of peaceful politics could never by themselves achieve a democratic resolution of the conflict because, as the facts of history showed, they had failed for centuries to do so.

In opposing this analysis, the supporters of the 'constitutional' approach also argued from the facts of history to show that the Nationalist failure to date to achieve a just and lasting settlement of the conflict (which included, they would say, the failure of militarist policies) was not due to any inherent deficiency in the methods of peaceful politics but to the internal divisions over strategy and tactics which had so often riven the approach of Nationalist leadership and policy.

In this century, for example, these divisions, which were directly related to the challenges of settling the conflict, had (according to the 'constitutional' analysis) engulfed the Irish nation in a continuous state of political civil war which had crippled its capacity for coherent and effective peacemaking.

Split down the middle by this internecine strife and confrontation, the Nationalist people of Ireland had been unable to organise a strategy which would have been equal to all the demands of settling the conflict in a peaceful and democratic way because it would have been energised by the full potential of their political resources at home and abroad.

In the view, then, of the 'constitutional' side of the dialogue, the Nationalist failure to date to settle the conflict was not due, in any inherent way, to the methods of peaceful politics. It was due rather to the fact, traceable through history, that Nationalist leadership and, consequently, the people whom they represented had never been able to deploy those methods with the efficacy necessary for success because they lacked the unity of vision and purpose which would alone have enabled them to do so.

Since the fundamental source of the efficacy of peaceful politics in a democratic society is the political will-power of the people who form it, it followed that the Nationalist people of Ireland could never respond effectively to all the challenges of democratic peacemaking in their own country unless and until they could face them through a strategy which focused the drive and thrust of a common vision and a common will.

Here, the advocates of the 'constitutional' argument pointed out that the only division which was now preventing the Nationalist people of Ireland from organising such a strategy was the one which had originally prompted the dialogue between the SDLP, Sinn Féin and the Irish Government: the division, namely, which still separated the adherents of the 'physical force' from the adherents of the 'constitutional' tradition.

If, however, the 'constitutional' side argued, this division could be healed by means of an agreement which would bring the two traditions together on the basis of a common or consensus strategy for the democratic resolution of the conflict, the peacemaking situation on the Nationalist side would be completely transformed. The Irish nation would then be able, for example, to exorcise the disunities which, in the past, had divided it against itself in the field of conflict resolution. It would also be able to develop a new spirit of peacemaking unity among its own people through which they could focus the full potential of their democratic resources at home and abroad on the tasks of bringing the blessings of peace to all those who in one traditional way or another regard Ireland as their homeland.

This was the thrust of the argument which finally persuaded the IRA to remove the 'physical dynamic' from the Nationalist side of the conflict by ending their campaign on a complete and definitive basis. It is vital to note the significance of, 1) the context and, 2) the thesis of that argument because of its importance for the future of peacemaking in Ireland. The *context* was a dialogue between two of the oldest and most bitterly opposed traditions in the history of Nationalist Ireland. The aim of the dialogue was to remove the gun forever from Nationalist politics on the basis of a new strategy for peace which would be driven towards its objective by the dynamics of peaceful and democratic politics.

The *thesis* accepted the principle that any realistic strategy for peacemaking in Ireland would have to contain a dynamic with the capacity to cope effectively with all the democratic issues which were at stake in the conflict.

It maintained that the Nationalist people of Ireland could develop such a dynamic provided, 1) they were in a position to organise a new peace strategy which would reflect their consensus on the democratic principles which should govern their approach to settling the conflict and provided also that, 2) the full efficacy of their political resources at home and abroad could be mobilised under their political leadership to support the implementation of that strategy.

It insisted that they would not be in a position to do that unless and until the supporters of both the 'constitutional' and the 'physical force' traditions became reconciled for the common good of all the people of Ireland on the basis of an agreement which reflected their consensus on the democratic principles which should govern the methods, the format, the dynamic and the overall objective of the proposed new strategy.

It also insisted, however, that, if such an agreement could be put in place, the Nationalist people of Ireland would be in a position to move forward towards a just and lasting settlement of the conflict on the basis of the peaceful and democratic dynamic described above.

This, then, distilled to its very essence, was the proposal for a new, 'alternative' strategy which would serve as the basis for ending the *raison d'être* of the 'physical force' tradition. It was put to the IRA on the understanding that, if they agreed to it, it would be implemented immediately by the Irish Government, the SDLP and Sinn Féin acting together on the basis of a consensus approach to the resolution of the conflict. In the end, they did so and, as a result, announced the cessation of the 31st of August, 1994. There is a direct relationship, therefore, between that cessation and the *implementation* of the new strategy. This relationship is at the heart of the Quid Pro Quo Understanding between the Irish Government, the SDLP and Sinn Féin which focuses and embodies the rapprochement between the 'physical force' and the 'constitutional' traditions. Since it is a *Quid Pro Quo* Understanding, it carries responsibilities, on the one hand, for the IRA and, on the other hand, for the Irish Government, the SDLP and Sinn Féin. The primary responsibility of the IRA is to be faithful to the terms of the cessation they announced on the 31st of August, 1994 while the primary responsibility of the leaderships of the Irish Government, the SDLP and Sinn Féin is to be faithful to the terms on which they agreed to respond to that cessation. These terms, which are set out in the Understanding, define the new *quid pro quo* strategy and the 'alternative dynamic' which would be its driving force.

All the leaderships concerned, namely, the Irish Government, the SDLP, Sinn Féin and the IRA are honour-bound to fulfil those responsibilities because honour is the bond of the Understanding.

Since these responsibilities are based on a *quid pro quo* or 'something for something' agreement, *the binding force* of the obligations they carry for one side of that agreement are related to *the fulfilment* of the obligations they carry for the other side of it.

This means, for example, that as long as the IRA are fulfilling their obligations to the Understanding, the Irish Government, the SDLP and Sinn Féin are bound in honour to fulfil the obligations it places on them. In the same way, as long as the Irish Government, the SDLP and Sinn Féin are doing that, the IRA are bound in honour to do the same.

In summary, then, the 'democratic consensus' between the Irish Government, the SDLP and Sinn Féin was that the 'alternative dynamic' of the new strategy would draw its efficacy as a peaceful and democratic driving force from the resources of the Irish nation at home and abroad when those resources had been harnessed under their consensus leadership to support the implementation of the strategy.

The principal democratic resource of the Irish nation is the political will-power of its own people when it has been focused by a common commitment to achieve a common goal under the direction of the leaderships they have elected to represent them. (This observation is a corollary of the principle that, in a democracy, the will of the people is the primary source of power.)

This means that the will of the Nationalist people of Ireland, North and South, focused by a common commitment to give their communal support to the aims and methods of the new strategy would constitute the peaceful and democratic driving force from which the 'alternative dynamic' would draw its political efficacy and power.

Unlike their compatriots in the Republic, the people of the Nationalist community in Northern Ireland are still directly entangled in the political conflict that has troubled the history of Ireland for centuries. They will remain entangled and consequently exposed to the threats it poses to their human and democratic dignity unless and until it has been resolved in a way that guarantees the protection of that dignity.

Due concern for their situation as a minority grouping locked into a political system which, historically, has been unjust to them requires that the approach to implementing the new strategy should take its primary focus from the peacemaking wishes they hold in common as those wishes are mediated through the leadership they have elected to represent them.

The fact that the age-old conflict is still alive in the political environment which surrounds them and that, consequently, they have to cope, day by day, with its real-life pressures means that their consensus backing is fundamental to the success and, indeed, to the very existence of the new strategy. This in turn means that the 'alternative dynamic' which drives the strategy must derive its fundamental efficacy and direction from the support they give in common to its implementation under the guidance of their own political leadership.

As the definition of the new strategy clearly implies, the support of the Nationalist people in the North would not of itself be enough to guarantee its success. For that reason, the leaderships of the SDLP, Sinn Féin and the Irish Government always accepted that the support of the people of the Republic mediated through the support of the Irish Government would also be necessary.

That is why the IRA cessation was based on the agreement, set out in the terms of the Quid Pro Quo Understanding, that the 'alternative dynamic' would derive its overall efficiency as the peaceful and democratic driving force of the new strategy from the combined support of the Nationalist people of Ireland, North and South.

The Overall Objective of the 'Democratic Consensus' Strategy

The overall objective of the 'democratic consensus' strategy is the democratic resolution of the conflict achieved through dialogue, negotiation and agreement between all the political parties with the necessary democratic mandate and the British and Irish Governments. The resolution of the conflict will take the form of a new political settlement which will respect and therefore accommodate the democratic rights of the people of both the Unionist and Nationalist traditions and create a healing environment for all the divided relationships which have been historically at the heart of the conflict.

The Inauguration of the 'Democratic Consensus' Strategy

It will be seen, then, from the account given here, that the meeting which took place on the 6th of September, 1994 between the then Taoiseach, Mr Albert Reynolds TD, the Leader of the SDLP, Mr John Hume MP MEP and the President of Sinn Féin, Mr Gerry Adams signified the successful culmination of the long process of peacemaking dialogue between two of the oldest and most divided traditions in the history of the Irish nation.

It was a unique moment, therefore, in that history since it symbolised the coming together of those two traditions in harmony and agreement on a new way forward to peace: a way that would be characterised by a 'democratic consensus' approach which would be inclusive of all the people of Ireland whatever their traditional background might be.

In effect, then, the meeting symbolised and sealed a new peace or covenant between the contemporary representatives of the 'physical force' and the 'constitutional' traditions of Nationalist Ireland. It had taken many years (some would say, centuries) to reach that moment but its arrival was signalled when the three leaders shook hands that day on the steps of Government Buildings in Dublin. The meeting marked a new departure, therefore, for Irish politics and the beginning of a new era in the history of the Irish nation. Consequently, its significance for peacemaking in Ireland could not be more profound or far-reaching. By symbolising the rapprochement between the two traditions, it signalled the healing of a schism in the Irish nation which, in this century particularly, had crippled its capacity to manage the challenges of peacemaking with the unity and focus needed for success.

This rapprochement was translated into practical terms by the Quid Pro Quo Understanding. That is why this Understanding became the joint basis for the IRA cessation and the meeting, five days later, between the three leaders.

The IRA leadership had confirmed their commitment to the Understanding by ending their campaign. It was agreed that, once they had done so, the other leaderships concerned would respond within a week in a public and ceremonial way that would carry the official stamp of their political authority as Head of the Irish Government, Leader of the SDLP and President of Sinn Féin. In other words, Mr Reynolds, Mr Hume and Mr Adams would come together as the political leaders of the Nationalist people of Ireland, North and South.

The purpose of their meeting would be to inaugurate the new, 'democratic alternative' strategy which, in accordance with the terms of the Quid Pro Quo Understanding, would serve as the *raison d'être* for the permanent removal of the 'physical force' dynamic from the Nationalist side of the conflict. Consequently, when Mr Reynolds, Mr Hume and Mr Adams met on the 6th of September, 1994, they were assembling in unison as the representative leadership of Nationalist Ireland to confirm and to place on public record their common commitment to implement the new, 'alternative' strategy as the permanent quid pro quo for the IRA cessation.

The meeting also dramatised the 'democratic consensus' which energises the 'alternative dynamic' of the new strategy. This means that, in a symbolic way, it proclaimed the fact that the Nationalist people of Ireland, North and South, were now in a position to organise a strategy which would be powerful enough to cope with all the demands of settling the conflict in a peaceful and democratic way because it would be energised by their resources at home and abroad, unified by a consensus leadership and supported by the dynamism of a common democratic vision and a common democratic will.

Meeting, then, as the representatives of Nationalist Ireland, the three leaders 'cut the tape', so to speak, on a new era in Nationalist politics: an era which would be characterised on the Nationalist side by a 'democratic consensus' approach to the resolution of the conflict and the consequent removal of the gun forever from Nationalist politics in Ireland.

However, to appreciate the full significance of what happened at that meeting, it is necessary to keep in mind that, in holding it, the three leaders concerned were acting with all the political and representative authority which belonged to their official positions as Taoiseach, Leader of the SDLP and President of Sinn Féin.

This gave the meeting a political and democratic status which needs to be clearly identified because of its implications for the binding force of the commitments made in and through it, particularly the commitment to implement the new, 'alternative' strategy in accordance with the consensus approach of the Quid Pro Quo Understanding. The factors which determined that status are as follows.

By taking part in the meeting as Taoiseach, Mr Reynolds was acting in his capacity as Head of the Irish Government and political leader of the people of the Republic. What he did, therefore, at the meeting, he did in the name of the Irish Government and also in the name of the people of the Republic. Mr Hume took part as the Leader of the SDLP. He was acting, therefore, on behalf of the SDLP and the people who had elected that party to represent them. This means that what he did at the meeting, he did in the name of the SDLP and the mandate of its electorate. In the same way, Mr Adams, by attending as the President of Sinn Féin, was acting officially on behalf of that party and the people it represents. What he did at the meeting, therefore, he did in the name of Sinn Féin and the mandate of its electorate.

The SDLP and Sinn Féin are the parties who together represent the Nationalist community in Northern Ireland. This means that, between them, they hold the democratic mandate of the people of that community and with it the authority to speak and act in their name.

It follows, then, that if and when Mr Hume and Mr Adams, as the respective leaders of the SDLP and Sinn Féin, agree between themselves to pursue together a course of action which is designed to achieve the common good of the Nationalist community they represent, their decision to do so carries the authority of the mandate of that community. In other words, whenever Mr Hume and Mr Adams decide together to exercise joint leadership of the Nationalist community in Northern Ireland in pursuit of a policy which represents the consensus of the parties they respectively lead, they are acting in the name and with the authority of that community. Since the due exercise of the office of Taoiseach carries the right to act in the name and with the authority of the Irish Government and the people whom they represent, it follows that if the Taoiseach, the Leader of the SDLP and the President of Sinn Féin were to pursue a joint policy for peace on the basis of an agreement between themselves which represented the consensus of the Irish Government, the SDLP and Sinn Féin, they would be acting in the name and with the authority of the people of the Republic and the people of the Nationalist community in the North.

These are the principles which defined the political and democratic status of the meeting under consideration. They show that the commitment to implement the new strategy given in and through it by the leaderships concerned is sanctioned by:

1. The authority vested in the Irish Government under the democratic mandate of the people of the Republic.
2. The authority vested in the SDLP and Sinn Féin under the democratic mandate of the people of the Nationalist community in Northern Ireland.

This means that the commitment is guaranteed by:

1. The good faith of the Irish Government and by implication, therefore (since it represents it), the good faith of the people of the Republic.
2. The good faith respectively of the SDLP and Sinn Féin and by implication, therefore (since they represent them), the good faith of the people of the Nationalist community in Northern Ireland.

It follows, therefore, that:

1. The Irish Government are bound by their word of honour (which embodies the word of honour of the people of Republic) to fulfil their responsibilities to that commitment.
2. The SDLP and Sinn Féin are also bound respectively by their word of honour (which embodies the word of honour of the people of the Nationalist community in Northern Ireland) to fulfil their responsibilities to that commitment.

This means that the obligation to implement the new 'alternative' strategy is based, respectively, on the word of honour of the Irish Government, the word of honour of the SDLP and the word of honour of Sinn Féin and by implication, therefore, the word of honour of all the people whom they represent.

In the same way, on the other side of the Quid Pro Quo Understanding, the obligation to implement the complete and definitive cessation of the IRA campaign is based on the word of honour of the IRA leadership and the people for whom they speak.

It will be seen, then, that the IRA did not call a cessation in a vacuum but in the context of a Quid Pro Quo Understanding, guaranteed on the word of honour of the Irish Government, the SDLP and Sinn Féin that, once their military campaign was completely and definitely ended, the new, peaceful strategy to achieve the democratic resolution of the conflict, based on a 'democratic consensus' approach by the Irish Government, the SDLP and Sinn Féin, would be immediately implemented.

Summary
In the light of the foregoing observations, the historical and political significance of the meeting between Mr Reynolds, Mr Hume and Mr Adams on the 6th of September, 1994 may be summarised as follows.

The meeting symbolised the inauguration of the new, consensus 'alternative' strategy which is the basis of the IRA cessation. This strategy is defined by the terms of the Quid Pro Quo Understanding. The meeting carried the pledge, publicly and solemnly given, that, on their word of honour, the Irish Government, the SDLP and Sinn Féin would faithfully fulfil their responsibilities to the Understanding, particularly their responsibility to maintain the implementation of the new strategy.

Taken together, the word of honour of the Irish Government, the SDLP and Sinn Féin represent the word of honour of the people of the Republic and the people of the Nationalist community in Northern Ireland because they (namely, the Irish Government, the SDLP and Sinn Féin) are the democratically mandated representatives of all those people.

The Understanding between the Irish Government, the SDLP and Sinn Féin on the one hand, and the IRA on the other, may be defined, therefore, as an accord, covenant or treaty, bonded by the word of honour of all the parties to it, and based on a commitment by the IRA to implement a cessation as the *quid pro quo* for a simultaneous commitment by the Irish Government, the SDLP and Sinn Féin to implement a new, peaceful 'alternative' strategy designed to achieve a truly democratic resolution of the conflict.

This Understanding represents the outcome of a long Nationalist dialogue which had to engage the human rights issues that are at the heart of the conflict, issues that have fuelled the forces of Irish history for centuries. It had also to cope with the tensions between the 'physical force' and 'constitutional' traditions that had divided the Irish nation against itself in its efforts to settle those issues in an efficacious and democratic way.

The Quid Pro Quo Understanding now marks the success of that dialogue because it embodies a rapprochement between the two traditions on the basis of the new, consensus strategy.

It is clear, therefore, from this background and, especially, from the *quid pro quo* nature of the Understanding that a conscious and deliberate decision to breach any of its fundamental terms by any of the major parties on either side of it would jeopardise its stability and, if that decision were to persist, it would inevitably cause the Understanding to disintegrate and collapse.

It follows that the commitment to implement an IRA cessation and the corresponding commitment to implement a new, democratic 'alternative' strategy are so interlocked that you cannot in fact have one without the other. They are of a piece and together they form the catalyst or dynamic which is holding the current peace process together. Consequently, if they fall asunder, the peace process itself will also fall asunder.

It may be truly said, therefore, that taken together these two commitments express the spirit of a common determination to remove the gun forever from Nationalist politics by means of a new, purely peaceful 'alternative' strategy for a truly democratic resolution for the conflict. As such, they form the bridge on which the 'constitutional' and the 'physical force' traditions of Irish history can be finally reconciled.

The following is the joint statement issued by the Taoiseach, Mr Albert Reynolds TD, the Leader of the SDLP, Mr John Hume MP MEP and the President of Sinn Féin, Mr Gerry Adams, on the 6th of September, 1994.

'We are at the beginning of a new era in which we are all totally and absolutely committed to democratic and peaceful methods of resolving our political problems. We reiterate that our objective is an equitable and lasting agreement that can command the allegiance of all. We see the Forum as a major instrument in that process. We reiterate that we cannot resolve this problem without the participation and agreement of the Unionist people. We call on everyone to use all their influence to bring this agreement about.'

17 December 1995
Document No. 4

THE TEST ISSUE OF THE PEACE PROCESS

Personal Note
In providing this commentary, I write as a participant in and a witness to all the discussions and all the communications, verbal and written, between the Irish Government and Sinn Féin, and also between the SDLP and Sinn Féin, which led eventually to the IRA cessation of 31st August 1994 and the meeting between the then Taoiseach, Mr Albert Reynolds TD, the leader of the SDLP, Mr John Hume MP and the President of Sinn Féin, Mr Gerry Adams at Government Buildings, Dublin on the 6th of September 1994.
Fr Alec Reid C.Ss.R.
Clonard Monastery,
Clonard Gardens,
Belfast BT13 2RL

The Test Issue of the Peace Process
The protection of the human and democratic dignity of the Nationalist community in Northern Ireland is the issue which is primarily at stake in the current phase of the peace process. The systematic suppression and oppression of that dignity during 50 years of Unionist and British controlled government in Northern Ireland to which the facts of history and the witness of those who lived through it testify ('the Nationalist nightmare' as it is sometimes called) point to the absolute need for such protection as an imperative of the democratic agenda for a just and lasting settlement.

How to provide it in a peaceful but effective way is, therefore, the crucial challenge which faces Nationalist leadership at the present time. It is clear that a negotiated settlement based on an agreement between all the parties to the conflict which would accommodate the democratic rights of the people of both the Nationalist and Unionist traditions in Ireland would be the best way to secure the dignity of the minority community in the North. In the absence of such a settlement and pending its achievement, an interim strategy to achieve the equality of treatment and parity of esteem which would protect that dignity must be put in place.

The design of this strategy in terms of the political principles which should govern its composition and the programme of tactical action through which it would seek to achieve its objective must, therefore, be regarded as issues of primary concern for Nationalist leadership at this stage of the peace process.

Given all the political circumstances, it is clear that the protection of the dignity and rights of the Nationalist community in Northern Ireland is a responsibility which must be shared between their leadership and the leadership of the Irish Government.

It follows that the practicalities of exercising this responsibility are matters for the consensus decision-making of both leaderships consulting and combining together in the light of whatever relevant issues are at stake.

The fact that Nationalist leadership in the North have first-hand personal and political experience of the plight and predicament of the Nationalist community there indicates that they are in the best position to advise on the formulation of any policy or programme designed to protect the dignity of that community.

They also constitute the political leadership which is directly mandated by the people of the Nationalist community in the North to protect and promote their political, social, economic and cultural interests. As such, they are answerable to those people for the faithful and effective discharge of those responsibilities.

The framework principle may be defined as follows: 'The people of the Nationalist community in Northern Ireland have the democratic right to equality of treatment and equality of esteem because of their human and democratic dignity as a community with their own historical, political and cultural identity.' As already noted, the common or consensus support of the people of the Nationalist community in the North is the fundamental dynamic of the strategy. Ultimately, the source of this dynamic is the most powerful democratic source of all, what may be described indeed as the very font of democracy – the respect which people have for their own dignity as people.

As a minority community in a political system originally designed to subdue them, Northern Nationalists on their own do not, however, have the necessary political potential to secure the permanent peaceful protection of their own dignity and rights. For that reason, the dynamic of the strategy must be empowered not only by their consensus support but also by the support of the Irish Government as the Sovereign Authority representing the people of the Republic.

That is why the commitment shared between the Irish Government, the SDLP and Sinn Féin to act in consort or unison on all issues which relate to the treatment of the Nationalist people of the North is the catalyst around which the full efficacy of the dynamic comes into focus. History, contemporary records and the *Realpolitik* of the situation show that, as a minority community subject, within the confines of a political society, to the fear and hostility of a majority one, Nationalists in Northern Ireland will remain vulnerable to the kind of persecution they have suffered in the past unless and until the protection of their dignity and rights has been secured by a new political settlement or, pending such a settlement, by the consensus strategy outlined above.

That is why the implementation of this strategy is an imperative of the peace process at the present time. Since co-operation between the Irish Government, the SDLP and Sinn Féin is at the heart of the strategy, arrangements to structure this co-operation are a *sine qua non* of its implementation.

A system to monitor, report and review what is actually happening in the here and now to the rights of Nationalists across the whole situation in Northern Ireland from government to street level needs to be in place so that the three leaderships concerned can maintain the kind of informed and 'hands on' approach which will enable them to take appropriate counter measures whenever it is clear that these rights are being neglected, damaged or violated.

At the end of the day, the real test of the political efficacy and the democratic integrity of the peace process will be whether or not it had the capacity to deliver the peaceful protection of Nationalist dignity in Northern Ireland.

Letter by Fr Alec Reid to Senator George Mitchell

18 November 1996
Clonard Monastery,
Clonard Gardens,
Belfast,
BT13 2RL

Dear Senator Mitchell,

I was hoping to see you in Belfast but as this may not be possible for another week at least and the matter is urgent, I have decided, after speaking to Martha, that I should write and forward this letter. It concerns the current opportunity for an unequivocal restoration of the 1994 IRA cessation and the circumstances which, since June last at least, have been not only delaying but threatening more and more to destroy it.

The gist of the situation is as follows. In what I would regard as a remarkable conversion from historical attitudes, the leaderships of both Sinn Féin and the IRA have now come to accept that the conflict here should be settled by the methods of peaceful and democratic politics. By this they mean a process of dialogue and negotiation between all the participants in the conflict leading to agreements and a consequent settlement which would accommodate the rights of all the participants. In other words, the leaderships of the Republican Movement are committed to a settlement, whatever form it might take, which had been negotiated through the methods of democratic conflict resolution as they are universally understood and practised. They are sceptical, however, (and this applies particularly to the IRA leadership) about the commitment of the British Government and the Unionist parties to the achievement of such a settlement. This scepticism is based on the failure, for whatever reason, of that Government and those parties over 18 months and after generations of conflict to seize the opportunity for a negotiated peace which was provided by the 1994 cessation.

It is important to understand the significance of that scepticism because it represents 'the critical mass', so to speak, which is now holding up another cessation. I can put this in another way by saying that the IRA remain to be convinced about the current willingness of either the British Government or, in particular, the Unionist parties to apply the dynamics of democratic politics to the resolution of the conflict.

Since the breakdown of the cessation in February last, the Sinn Féin leadership have been engaged in several initiatives to restore it. The latest of these began in June last when, through the good offices of John Hume, Gerry Adams sent a written and verbal message to the British Prime Minister requesting assurances on three specific issues which, if they were provided, would place him in a position to persuade the IRA to establish an unequivocal restoration of the 1994 cessation.

To date, however, these assurances have not been given in a way that would enable Mr Adams to proceed. They relate to the following issues.

1. The entrance of Sinn Féin into the current peace talks without any precondition beyond the unequivocal restoration of the 1994 cessation. This applies, in particular, to any preconditions about decommissioning.
2. An agreed time frame for the conduct of negotiations which would focus the agenda in a business-like way and so engender the momentum for real and constructive progress towards a settlement.
3. A programme of measures to be undertaken by the British Government on issues like the treatment of the Nationalist community, the release of prisoners and the repeal of emergency legislation which would help to rebuild Republican confidence in the efficacy of the peace process in so far as it depends on the commitment and good faith of that Government.

The idea behind the initiative is that the British Government would make a statement outlining their commitment to a negotiated settlement and providing the three specific assurances requested by Sinn Féin. Then, by prior arrangement and within a matter of hours, the IRA would respond by declaring an unequivocal restoration of the 1994 complete cessation.

The communication, facilitated by Mr Hume, through which the initiative is being carried forward has now been ongoing for almost four months but there are still critical gaps between the British and Sinn Féin positions on the three issues listed above. Indeed, a new issue, relating to the timing of Sinn Féin's entrance to the talks after an IRA cessation, has now arisen to divide them even further.

While the British Government have been responding through Mr Hume to Sinn Féin's requests, they have so far failed to do so in a way that would enable the Sinn Féin leadership to deliver a new cessation. The Sinn Féin position on decommissioning is that it should be addressed and resolved in accordance with the principles and recommendations of the International Body's report. Beyond that they are not prepared to go and so they will continue to insist that they should not be subject to any preconditions arising from the issue of decommissioning either before or during their participation in the negotiations. It is not possible to deliver an IRA cessation on the basis of the current British approach to that issue. It would, however, be possible if the British Government's approach were in keeping with the Sinn Féin approach outlined above. In Sinn Féin's view, such an agreed approach could be expressed as follows. 'Among the crucial issues is decommissioning which must be resolved without blocking the negotiations. So the opening plenary will address the International Body's proposals on decommissioning of illegal arms. At that stage and without blocking the negotiations, the British Government, along with the Irish Government, will be looking for the commitment of all participants to work constructively during the negotiations to implement all aspects of the International Body's report.'

The second gap between the two sides relates to a time frame and calendar for the conduct of negotiations. Sinn Féin say that, in accordance with the principles of efficient management, the talks must be organised on the basis of a dynamic time frame which, by focusing the minds and concentrating the energies of the participants, would generate the momentum that will be necessary for progress and ultimate success. They maintain, therefore, that, on such a crucial issue, the British and Irish Governments must take the lead by agreeing together on a time frame and then by proposing it to the participants for their agreement and adoption. They point out that the two Governments have already taken such a lead in relation to a number of issues including both the chairing of the talks and the ground rules for the talks and that the alternative to their doing so is the kind of stalling and obstruction which has so often characterised the negotiations to date.

Sinn Féin propose a concentrated time frame of six months and it is worth noting that, in a recent public statement, Mr John Hume agreed with them.

The British Government's position, as communicated to Sinn Féin, is that they want the negotiations to proceed to a successful outcome as speedily as possible but that they cannot control the time frame. They are prepared, however, to encourage the participants to adopt an agreed indicative time frame for the conduct of negotiations and, at the same time, to pursue an agenda for reviewing progress through a plenary session of the talks and also through meetings at the highest level between the representatives of both Governments.

In response, Sinn Féin say that this approach is not dynamic enough because it lacks the leadership which both Governments must give if the talks are to move forward effectively towards a settlement. Consequently, the Governments must have a position of their own on a time frame and calendar and they must then promote it in a public and proactive way in order to persuade the participants to agree to it. To reduce the Government input on the issue to a policy of encouraging the participants to agree among themselves on a time frame and calendar would, in Sinn Féin's view, be a recipe for inefficiency, filibustering and ultimate failure because it would not move the Unionist parties to co-operate. It will not be possible to deliver an IRA cessation on the basis of the current British approach to a time frame and calendar. It would, however, be possible if the British Government were to agree in principle with the Sinn Féin approach outlined above. In Sinn Féin's view, such an agreed approach could be expressed as follows.

'The British Government is determined to see these negotiations through successfully as speedily as possible. The British and Irish Governments are together committed to an agreed time frame and calendar for the conduct of the negotiations which we will propose to the participants and encourage them to adopt. We have already proposed that a plenary meeting should be held at a suitable date to take stock of progress in the negotiating as a whole. The two Governments will also review progress at regular intervals including a summit meeting to be held before the end of the year.'

The third gap relates to measures for building confidence. Here, Sinn Féin say that the failure of the British Government to organise peace talks during the 18 months of the IRA cessation has undermined Republican confidence in the sincerity of their commitment to a process of genuine peacemaking. Consequently, they are asking the British Government to commit itself to a programme of measures relating to the treatment of the Nationalist community and to sensitive Republican concerns like the release of prisoners which, if carried through in the event of another IRA cessation, would, in Sinn Féin's view, help to restore that confidence.

They are looking for a specific rather than a general commitment in the sense that they want the British Government to spell out the practical steps they would take to implement such a programme. Since it might not be feasible for them to do that in public, it would be sufficient if they were to indicate in confidence to an independent witness like Mr John Hume or the Irish Government what those practical steps would be.

The issues which, in Sinn Féin's view, need to be addressed as part of a programme of confidence building measures are:

1. Those issues which fall into the equality and democratic rights agenda and which address political, economic, social and cultural discrimination. Sinn Féin say that these issues do not require any negotiation and that consequently they can and should be addressed immediately. The principles of equality of treatment, equality of opportunity and parity of esteem would have to apply across the political, cultural, economic, social, legal and security spectrum. These would include:
   • Equality of opportunity in employment.
   • Equality of treatment for the Irish culture and identity.
   • Equality of treatment of elected representatives.
   • Equality in the provision of education, specifically through the medium of Irish.
   • Equality of treatment in economic development.
2. In the event of a new IRA cessation, issues like the release of prisoners and the repeal of emergency legislation would also have to be addressed in a programmatic way by the agenda for confidence building. The British Government have told Sinn Féin through Mr Hume that they are committed to the principle of confidence building and that consequently they will continue to pursue social and economic policies based on the principles of equality of opportunity, equity of treatment and parity of esteem irrespective of political, cultural or religious affiliation or gender. They have also referred to the confidence building measures like new arrangements for the release of prisoners and the removal of the security forces from the streets which were put in place after the 1994 cessation.

They also make the point, which Sinn Féin accept, that confidence building is a two-way street.

In response, Sinn Féin say that the British commitment is not specific enough. If they are to fulfil their own role in the initiative successfully, they need to know the detail of the actual programme through which the British Government will follow through on their general commitment to confidence building. This request is in keeping with Sinn Féin's whole approach to the initiative when they say that verbal commitments must be backed by explanations of how and when they will be implemented in practice. Since the initiative began in June, Sinn Féin have acted on the understanding given to them by the British and Irish Governments when they said on February 28th last that the only condition for their entrance to the talks was 'an unequivocal restoration of the complete cessation of August 1994'. To make sure that this understanding was correct, they sought and received verification of it from both Governments.

They now find, however, that the British Government have changed their position on the issue because, in a communication forwarded through Mr Hume in September, they say, in effect, that Sinn Féin will be allowed entrance to the peace talks after an IRA cessation provided that they (the British Government) are sure, after consideration and in view particularly of events on the ground, that the cessation is genuinely unequivocal. Sinn Féin say that this position is contrary to the understanding given to them by both Governments of what was required for their admittance to the talks in a way that amounts to a new precondition. They say this because to accept it would, in their view, make that admittance dependent not only on an unequivocal IRA cessation but also on a decision which the British Government would be free to make in their time and at their own discretion. If this approach to the timing of Sinn Féin's participation in the talks were to be implemented, it would undermine the whole basis of the current initiative as Sinn Féin understand it and so destroy the efforts they have made so far to deliver a new IRA cessation. It would also create a new wellspring for the kind of difficulties which have bedevilled the peace process for the past two years. Consequently, for those reasons, it is unacceptable to Sinn Féin.

Comments in the media suggesting a three-months' gap between an IRA cessation and Sinn Féin's entrance to the peace talks and coming, Sinn Féin believe, from British sources, together with statements from the Secretary of State, have confirmed Sinn Féin's suspicions that the British Government are deliberately raising the bar on their participation in the negotiations. While Sinn Féin would accept a timing for their entrance which would conform to a 'business as usual' timetable at the talks, they will not agree to any other timing that would go beyond that of an unequivocal IRA cessation, all the more if it carried the connotations of a 'decontamination' period. In relation to this issue, Sinn Féin say that an IRA cessation will only be deliverable on the basis of a commitment from the British Government that Sinn Féin will be admitted to the peace talks immediately and without any preconditions once the IRA have declared an unequivocal restoration of the 1994 cessation.

I believe that, in the light of all the circumstances, the Sinn Féin approach set out above is a reasonable one. It is significant that Mr John Hume agrees with it and that the Irish Government, from what I have been told, have indicated to the American Government that they too 'could sign up to it'. This suggests that the Sinn Féin approach is supported by a consensus on the Nationalist side.

It is not, in my opinion, too much to say that the historical Irish conflict is now moving towards a climax in a context which has the potential for a peace that would be better and a war that would be worse than ever before. I believe, however, that peace will win out if, with the help of God, the situation is managed with the necessary skill, courage and determination. But time is running out and the current initiative may be our last chance this side of civil war. We have reached a point, therefore, where decisions must be made by the parties concerned. Otherwise, the opportunity that now exists will evaporate and disappear.

Sinn Féin have been doing all they can to create the conditions for a new IRA cessation but their efforts have now reached the point of exhaustion. I say this from a position where I have been kept fully informed about everything that is happening. Here, it is important to keep in mind that, however related they may be by politics and history, Sinn Féin and the IRA are separate organisations. This means that Sinn Féin cannot tell the IRA what to do because, at the end of the day, the IRA will make their own assessments and take their own decisions. Whether one likes this or not, it is, unfortunately, the *Realpolitik* of the situation which Sinn Féin have to manage.

On the 10th of October last, Sinn Féin forwarded a proposal to the British Government on the lines described above but to date they have received no official response to it. They know, however, that the British Government have been consulting the Irish Government about it for the past fortnight or so because the Irish Government are keeping them informed.

Given that the Sinn Féin proposal is a reasonable one, it will, in their view, test the willingness of the British Government and the Unionist parties to work effectively for a negotiated settlement. Sinn Féin and the IRA want a negotiated settlement because they believe that it alone could finally secure the equality that is due in justice to the people of the Nationalist community. Any other arrangement would, in their view, maintain the substance of the old status quo and so leave the Nationalist community vulnerable to the kind of inequality and oppression it suffered in the past. In other words, it would be a pseudo settlement which could produce little more than a cosmetic peace.

For Sinn Féin, then, everything turns on whether or not the British Government are truly committed to a negotiated settlement because, as the ruling authority, they hold the decisive power. They decided, therefore, to search out the character of that commitment through their proposal of October 10th. The acid test in that proposal is their suggestion for a time frame because, in effect, it is also their suggestion for a dynamic which would have the capacity to focus the peace negotiations and to move them forward in an efficient way towards a negotiated settlement. If the British Government are truly committed to such a settlement, they must in consequence accept the need for such a dynamic and the time frame that would embody it. That is the logic of the Sinn Féin test and why the British Government's response to their proposal and, in particular, to their suggestion for the implementation of a time frame is so crucial to another cessation. If the British Government's response is positive, Sinn Féin will be in a position to persuade the IRA that their commitment to a negotiated settlement is genuine and, once they are able to do that, they will also be able to persuade them to declare an unequivocal restoration of the 1994 cessation.

The willingness or otherwise of the British Government to accept the Sinn Féin proposal for a dynamic time frame for the conduct of the peace talks is the issue, therefore, on which, more than any other, the current initiative will stand or fall. There is no need to develop this point further because I know you will understand its implications for the peace process at a time when it is at a crossroads defined on the one side by so much opportunity and on the other by so much danger.

I trust that this letter will help you to understand how the current initiative has been developing and how it stands at this date. I am sorry that it is so long but I know you would want me to explain everything as clearly as possible. I know also that Sinn Féin would want me to do so because they place a lot of trust in your ability and in your willingness to help.

I send personal and prayerful good wishes for your health, welfare and the success of your efforts to bring peace to Ireland.
With kindest regards,
Yours sincerely,
Alex Reid C.Ss.R.

Endnotes

1   See, for instance, D. McKittrick and D. McVea, *Making Sense of the Troubles: A History of the Northern Ireland Conflict* (London: Viking/Penguin, 2012); E. Mallie and D. McKittrick, *The Fight for Peace: The Secret Story Behind the Irish Peace Process* (London: Heinemann, 1996); J. Powell, *Great Hatred, Little Room: Making Peace in Northern Ireland* (London: Bodley Head, 2008); J.B. Bell, *The Irish Troubles: A Generation of Violence, 1967–1992* (Dublin: Gill and Macmillan, 1993); T.P. Coogan, *The Troubles: Ireland's Ordeal, 1966–1996 and the Search for Peace* (London: Hutchinson, 1995); J. Holland, *Hope Against History: The Ulster Conflict* (London: Coronet Lir Books, 1999); D. de Bréadún, *The Far Side of Revenge: Making Peace in Northern Ireland* (Cork: Collins Press, 2001).

2   Existing brief accounts of this ministry include: D. Little (ed.), *Peacemakers in Action: Profiles of Religion in Conflict Resolution* (New York: Tanenbaum Center for Interreligious Understanding, 2007); J. Brewer, G.I. Higgins and F. Teeney, *Religion, Civil Society and Peace in Northern Ireland* (Oxford: Oxford University Press, 2012).

3   These interviews were conducted by the then provincial superior of the Irish Redemptorists, Fr Michael Kelleher C.Ss.R. In this essay they will be referred to by the title given to the transcribed version in the archive of the Dublin Province: 'Interview Kelleher–Reid'.

4   The author is grateful to the following for agreeing to be interviewed: Gerry Adams, Brendan Callanan, Harold Good, Ken Newell, Martin Mansergh, Martin McGuinness, Alec Reid, Derek Poole and Gerry Reynolds. These interviews will be referred to in the notes as: Interview McKeever–Adams, Interview McKeever–Callanan, etc.

5   Martin Mansergh confirms that Fr Alec's role was most important in the years between 1987 and 1994, but that it was also vital in re-establishing the ceasefire in 1997 (Interview McKeever–Mansergh).

6   A familiar slogan used at the time by those who sought equality of civil rights was 'One man, one vote!' This is one of the resonances associated with the title of this book. Other possible resonances are the loneliness of Fr Alec's journey and his strong conviction that peace for all could be found in the one God.

7   Fr Alec affirms that he was ordained in 1957, appointed briefly to Esker, a Redemptorist community in the west of Ireland, then to Dundalk, and then 'in 1961 or 1962' to Belfast (Interview Kelleher–Reid).

8   This history has been studied in detail by J. Grant, *One Hundred Years With the Clonard Redemptorists* (Dublin: Columba Press, 2003); see particularly chapters 1 and 13.

9   To this day the strength of these bonds is brought out each year in June during the 'Clonard Novena', nine days of prayer attended by many thousands of people from all over Belfast and beyond.

10 Interview McKeever–Reid.

11 In recalling his encounter with the Traveller, Fr Alec uses a phrase that we will meet later as regards his peace ministry: 'something should be done about this' (Interview Kelleher–Reid).

12 'I also met with Mr Scott and Lord Mayhew and had contact with Lord Melchet and Lord Elton, who were all Secretaries of State for Northern Ireland' (Interview Kelleher–Reid).

13   Unless otherwise indicated, all indented quotations of this kind are taken from Interview Kelleher–Reid. This indication will not be given anew each time.

14   The affection in which Fr Alec held such women comes out in this little anecdote about a lady outside a room in which one of the early ecumenical meetings was taking place: 'One of the helpers, a wonderful person from the Falls Road, who had a great sense of humour, used to say when the discussions were taking place "There they are in there airing their intelligences"' (Interview Kelleher–Reid).

15   'But Gusty [Spence] and I became firm friends, he was a leader and we were real friends. Then there was the leader of the Red Hand Commandos and he was blamed for leading the burning of Bombay Street, this particular Loyalist. I remember when he came on television I used to stand up and walk off because I blamed him for burning Bombay Street, but, whatever the circumstances were, I became friendly with him. I was also friendly with David Irvine, who would have been more publicly known' (Interview Kelleher–Reid).

16   As the story of Fr Alec's ministry emerges we will have occasion to note what is happening on the other side of the peace line.

17   '... But my mother was Cumann na mBan in the war of independence; a very strong republican; very strong and made no secret of it' (Interview Kelleher–Reid).

18   Ken Newell, a Presbyterian minister much involved in reconciliation work, explains that Fr Alec 'understood the republican mindset' and so was able to engage with republicans in the quest for peace (Interview McKeever–Newell).

19   Interview Kelleher–Reid.

20   This came out in an exaggerated form, in 2005, in his famous comparison of the unionists with the Nazis, for which Fr Alec later apologised.

21   Interview McKeever–Newell.

22   Interview Kelleher–Reid.

23   On this day the Parachute Regiment shot dead thirteen unarmed civilians. Falsely denied by the Widgery report, this fact was only publicly acknowledged by the British government after the Saville Inquiry in 2010. It is an interesting historical fact that, while the IRA were in no way involved in this violence, one of the commanders in Derry that day was Martin McGuinness.

24   Fr Alec recounts how, on one occasion, after the IRA had thrown a blast bomb over the peace line, he asked to meet the local commanders. At the meeting they explained that this had been to frighten off a group who looked as if they were going to attack the Clonard area (Interview Kelleher–Reid).

25   Looking back on this form of collaboration, Gerry Adams recalls: 'In the wake of the 1977 inter-republican feuding, Fr Reid and Fr Des [Wilson] succeeded in establishing an arbitration and mediation process between different republican organisations'; G. Adams, *Hope and History* (London/Dingle: Brandon Press, 2003), p. 6.

26   'It was Fr Reid who suggested that we meet with Cardinal Ó Fiaich on the prison issue, and myself, Fr Des, Danny Morrison and Kevin Hannaway travelled regularly to Ara Coeli – the Primate's residence in Armagh – to discuss the situation'; Adams, *Hope and History*, p. 8.

27   'On one occasion Colette and I found him in a very distressed state as the health of the hunger strikers deteriorated. Paradoxically, while the plight of the prisoners and their families and the ongoing conflict continued to wear him down, he took great comfort from the messages of support that the imprisoned men had smuggled out to him'; Adams, *Hope and History*, p. 9.

28 For insight into changed thinking among loyalist paramilitaries, see R. Garland, *Gusty Spence* (Belfast: Blackstaff Press, 2001). Among Protestant clergy, Derek Poole has followed closely the evolution of loyalism. He is particularly interested in the nature of sectarianism, which he calls 'identity gone wrong'; Interview McKeever–Poole.

29 See M. Mansergh, 'The legacy of the hunger strikes', in idem, *The Legacy of History* (Cork: Mercier Press, 2003), pp. 405–8.

30 Interview Kelleher–Reid.

31 On quite a number of occasions in the interviews, while recalling particular events, Fr Alec expresses regret about what he should have done. This is a characteristic which Harold Good defines as 'inappropriate guilt' (Interview McKeever–Good).

32 'My whole involvement in the peace process and all that kind of thing I did on my own initiative; I wasn't told by any Superior to get involved in peacemaking' (Interview Kelleher–Reid).

33 'So my objective was to stop people being killed and it was the objective of the Redemptorists, because anything I did, I have to say, I did it as a Redemptorist and with the backing of the Redemptorists' (Interview Kelleher–Reid).

34 In an interview with F. Teeney, Bishop Edward Daly describes Fr Alec's position as follows: 'Alec wanted to be free of any control, acting as an independent agent. But at the same time he wasn't acting unknown to us, at least not to Cahal Daly, but Tom Ó Fiaich and myself were very much involved.'

35 Martin Mansergh perceives Fr Alec Reid as someone 'who was attempting to save the honour of the institution he represented' (Interview McKeever–Mansergh).

36 The importance of this key moment is recalled by Gerry Adams as follows: 'However, I put to him my view that armed struggle occurs in the absence of an alternative way to bring about conditions of justice and equality. The focus, therefore, of those wishing to see an end to armed struggle had to be on building this alternative'; Adams, *Hope and History*, p. 29.

37 This fact was confirmed by Gerry Adams, who talks of Fr Alec as a 'conduit' between the concerned parties (Interview McKeever–Adams).

38 From Fr Alec's point of view, 1986 was quite an advanced stage in his involvement, which he normally dates from the early 1970s. The following comment helps us appreciate the difficulty of the long years before this new, more successful, phase of the peace process: 'Well, I suppose in the early days, really, it was very, very, frustrating you know. Because we tried, from about 1972 when it started, I think we must have tried about ten different initiatives, some of them involving Loyalists. An initiative would take six or nine months to get it together and they all collapsed. You were kind of trying to walk up the wall there, that kind of thing. You went through nine or ten different kind of initiatives and it was all to try to persuade the IRA to stop and that was over a period of around ten years without success' (Interview Kelleher–Reid).

39 In an interview with K. Rafter in 2002, Fr Alec makes this point as follows: 'One of the things I discovered very quickly was that the people who most wanted peace were the IRA. Who wants to live that kind of life, always on the run? These were young men in their early twenties, with wives and young children, caught up in nightmare stuff. They wanted some way of getting out of that honourably'; quoted in K. Rafter, *Sinn Féin 1905–2005: In the Shadow of Gunmen* (Dublin: Gill & Macmillan, 2005), p. 172.

40 When the talks became publicly known, both men paid a high price for their efforts: 'However, our talks became public in 1993 and the resultant pressures and vilifications were awful, making life extremely difficult for both of us'; J. Hume, *A New Ireland:*

Politics, Peace, and Reconciliation (Boulder, CO: Roberts Rinehart Publishers, 1996), p. 116.

41　The key contribution of Mansergh to the peace process is studied in K. Rafter, *Martin Mansergh: A Biography* (Dublin: New Island, 2002).

42　It is important to remember that while Martin Mansergh was the key contact between Dublin and the republicans for many years, this certainly does not mean that he was the only one on the Dublin scene who contributed to the peace process.

43　The details of this accord can be found in document 2 of Fr Alec's submission to the International Body in 1995, reproduced in the Documentation section of this book.

44　Interview Kelleher–Reid.

45　The full text is available in the Documentation section of this book.

46　See the funeral reflection of Fr Michael Kelleher in the Testimonials section of this book.

47　Interview Kelleher–Reid.

48　It is interesting to read the reflections of different participants concerning meetings of this kind, which went on in different forms right through the Troubles. Gerry Adams, for instance, makes this interesting comment: 'I found these engagements energising and thought-provoking … All were unionists, mainly with a small 'u'. They had never been subjected to republican arguments. Few if any of us had been subjected to unionist arguments, and as we developed our peace strategy these discussions informed our deliberations'; Adams, *Hope and History*, p. 15. From the other side of the fence, someone like Ken Newell offers this reflection: 'The input of one of the republicans was fairly static – you were talking to an answering machine, it was set in concrete. That was the view eighteen months into our talks: we had reached an impasse … In Spring 1992 we noticed Sinn Féin were prepared to make peace … There was a feeling of a genuine willingness to try to make peace on the basis of the principles of self-determination of the Irish people, consent, and a democratic resolution of the conflict. There was a new agenda. In quite another vein, but not without its symbolic importance, Harold Good remembers the strange impression it made on him the first time Gerry Adams served him a cup of tea!' Interview McKeever–Good.

49　For an interesting account of these talks, including the perspective of Austin Currie as one of the SDLP delegation, see Mallie and McKittrick, *The Fight for Peace*, pp. 79–82.

50　Interview McKeever–Reynolds.

51　For technical details on these documents, see J. Tonge, *Northern Ireland: Conflict and Change*, 2nd edn. (Harlow, Essex: Pearson Education, 2002), pp. 158–62.

52　Interestingly and importantly, in the body of the documents Fr Alec Reid describes himself as 'a participant in and a witness to' these discussions.

53　Looking back on the peace process as a whole, Gerry Adams has no doubt that Fr Alec Reid should be 'right up there' among those who made the process possible; Interview McKeever–Adams.

54　For this reason Fr Alec disapproved of the term 'pan-Nationalist front' (Interview McKeever–Reid).

55　Interview Kelleher–Reid.

56　The text of the lecture is available in the Documentation section of this book.

Select Bibliography

Adams, G., *Hope and History: Making Peace in Ireland* (Dingle/London: Brandon, 2003)

Bell, J. B., *The Irish Troubles: A Generation of Violence, 1967–1992* (Dublin: Gill & Macmillan, 1993)

Brewer J., Higgins, G.I and Teeney, F., *Religion, Civil Society and Peace in Northern Ireland* (Oxford: Oxford University Press, 2012)

Coogan, T. P., *The Troubles: Ireland's Ordeal 1966–1996 and the Search for Peace* (London: Hutchinson, 1995)

de Bréadún, D., *The Far Side of Revenge: Making Peace in Northern Ireland* (Cork: Collins Press, 2001)

Garland, R., *Gusty Spence* (Belfast: Blackstaff Press, 2001)

Grant, J., *One Hundred Years With the Clonard Redemptorists* (Dublin: Columba Press, 2003)

Hume, J., *A New Ireland: Politics, Peace, and Reconciliation* (Boulder, CO: Roberts Rinehart Publishers, 1996)

Holland, J., *Hope Against History: The Ulster Conflict* (London: Coronet Lir Books, 1999)

Little, D. (ed.), *Peacemakers in Action: Profiles of Religion in Conflict Resolution* (New York: Tanenbaum Center for Interreligious Understanding, 2007)

MacMánais, R., *The Road from Ardoyne: The Making of a President* (Dingle/London: Brandon, 2004)

Moloney, E., *A Secret History of the IRA* (London: Allen Lane/Penguin, 2002)

Mallie, E. and McKittrick, D., *The Fight for Peace* (London: Heinemann, 1996)

Mallie, E. and McKittrick, D., *Endgame in Ireland* (London: Hodder and Stoughton, 2001)

Mansergh, M., *The Legacy of History* (Cork: Mercier Press, 2003)

McKittrick, D. and McVea, D., *Making Sense of the Troubles: A History of the Northern Ireland Conflict* (London: Viking/Penguin, 2012)

Murray, G. and Tonge, J., *Sinn Féin and the SDLP: From Alienation to Participation* (Dublin: O'Brien Press, 2005)

O'Clery, C., *The Greening of the White House: The Inside History of How America Tried to Bring Peace to Ireland* (Dublin: Gill & MacMillan, 1996)

Powell, J., *Great Hatred, Little Room: Making Peace in Northern Ireland* (London: Bodley Head, 2008)

Rafter, K., *Sinn Féin 1905–2005: In the Shadow of Gunmen* (Dublin: Gill & Macmillan, 2005)

Rafter, K., *Martin Mansergh: A Biography* (Dublin: New Island, 2002)

Rowan, B., *Behind the Lines: The Story of the IRA and Loyalist Ceasefires* (Belfast: Blackstaff Press, 1995)

Tonge, J., *Northern Ireland: Conflict and Change*, 2nd edn. (Harlow, Essex: Pearson Education Limited, 2002)